CHOICES

Helping Keep Up Their Quality of Life

KNOLL PHARMA INC.

In memory of the people who taught me about choices:

Johannes Fernandus Gerardus van Bommel
Jacoba Christina Henrica Maria van Bommel — van Enckevort
Franciscus Hubertus van Enckevort

and dedicated to my family who shared in their loss but also in their lessons:

Janet Klees
Rieky, Hubert, Sonja and Jan Alexander Haas
Philo van Enckevort
the van Ryswyk family
the van Soest family
Trevor Man
and the Man family.

CHOICES

FOR PEOPLE WHO HAVE A TERMINAL ILLNESS THEIR FAMILIES AND THEIR CAREGIVERS

HARRY VAN BOMMEL

NC PRESS LIMITED

To contact author for speaking engagements, write:
PSD Consultants,
11 Miniot Circle,
Scarboro, ON, Canada
M1K 2K1
(416) 264-4665

Fourth Printing, 1993.
Third Printing, 1989.
© Harry van Bommel 1987, Second Revised Edition.
No part of this publication may be reproduced, stored in a
retrieval system, or transmitted, in any form or by any means,
electronic, mechanical, photocopying, recording or otherwise,
without the prior written permission of NC Press Limited.

DISCLAIMER: KNOLL is pleased to sponsor this reprinting of *CHOICES*.
The views expressed herein are those of the author and not of this firm.

Canadian Cataloguing in Publication Data

van Bommel, Harry
   Choices : for people who have a terminal illness,
their families and their caregivers

ISBN 1-055021-054-8

I. Terminal care. 2. Terminally ill. I. Title

R726.8.V32   1989   362.1'75   C89-094391-5

We would like to thank the Ontario Arts Council, the Ontario Publishing
Centre, the Ontario Ministry of Culture and Communications, Department of
Communications, Canada, and the Canada Council for their assistance in the
production of this book.

New Canada Publications, a division of NC Press Limited, Box
452, Station A, Toronto, Ontario, Canada, M5W 1H8.

Printed and bound in Canada

CONTENTS

ACKNOWLEDGMENTS

This book examines nine major topics and required the help and encouragement of many people. Although numerous people are mentioned in this section, each individual's contribution was very important.

I thank all the people at NC Press for their efforts: **Caroline Walker, Janet Walker, Elizabeth Whitehead, Lisa Dimson, Elina Guttenberg, Lynn McClory, Ron Lovering, Rani Gill and Ruth Chernia.**

My heartfelt thanks to the people who shared their personal stories with me: **Estelle Altman, Ph.D.; Carol Brock, M.D.; Frances Elliott, R.N.; The Reverend Keith Nevel; Hans Peters; and Jane and John Rogers.**

The following people and organizations provided information and assistance for which I am grateful: **American Civil Liberties Union, Anglican Book Centre; The Connecticut Hospice Inc.; Malin Kurz; Joe Gilhooly and Edward W. Keyserlingk, Law Reform Commission of Canada; The Medical Post; New York Task Force on Life and the Law; St. Christopher's Hospice; John Toye; and Carol Willimus** plus many of the organizations listed in the Appendix.

I want to thank all the people I interviewed throughout the research for this book, with special thanks to the following people: **Nell Bushby** of the Bessie Dane Foundation (Hospice Program on Salt Spring Island, B.C.); **Marcia Darling,** Manager of Marketing Services for the Toronto Trust Cemeteries; **Mary Devassy, M.D.,** a Family Practitioner; **Jo Dixon, Llona O'Gorman** and **Marie Teitge** of Hospice Victoria; **Stephen Fleming, Ph.D.,** a psychologist with expertise in palliative care; **Peter Hanson, M.D.,** author; **Bob Hatfield, M.D.** and **Diane Yackel** of Hospice Calgary; **Paul Henteleff, M.D.,** Director of the Palliative Care Unit, St. Boniface Hospital, Winnipeg, Manitoba; **Derek Humphry,** Executive Director of the Hemlock Society; **Dorothy C. H. Ley, M.D., F.R.C.P.(C), F.A.C.P.,** Executive Director of the Palliative Care Foundation; and **Ken Walker, M.D.,** author.

Several people read most or all of the manuscript and provided very useful suggestions for improvements: **Estelle Altman, Ph.D.; Leslie Balmer; Carol Brock, M.D.; Colleen Burns, Janet Klees and Bill Weiss, M.D.** Any content errors that remain are mine.

Special thanks to the following people for their help with this revised edition: **Dr. Balfour Mount, M.D., F.R.C.S.(C),** Director, Palliative Care Service, Professor of Surgery, McGill University, **Dame Cicely Saunders, DBE, F.R.C.P., F.R.C.S.,** founder St. Christopher's Hospice, London, **Derek Humphry, Warner Montgomery,** and **Rieky Haas.**

Authors who work a long time to prepare a book often need the support and encouragement of their family and friends to make that work possible. Aside from some of the people previously mentioned I would like to thank the following people for their present encouragement and, also, for their support and help during my parents and grandfather's illnesses: **Ricarda Amberg; Leslie Balmer; Julie Benson; Stephen Campbell; Hung Der, D.D.S.; Trevor Man; Mary Mocak, B.Sc.Phm.; Josi Perotto; Tom Warney** and the following families: **Berkhof, Camps, Genova, Haas, Hermsen, Hudkins, Huson, Ingenpas, Keursten, Kelly, Klees, Lenssen, Man, McGhee, Moerman, Morley, Novicevic, Rochard, Stofberg, Teunissen, Shakespeare, van Bommel, van Enckevort, van Gaal, van Ginkel, van Ryswyk, van Soest, Wammes, Wilmsen, Wttewaall,** and **Young.**

My loving thanks to my best friend, **Janet,** for always being there.

INTRODUCTION

This book is designed for people who have a terminal illness, their families and caregivers (e.g. physicians, nurses, clerics, therapists, volunteers). Its purpose is simply to provide an overview of the choices available to everyone, while at the same time encouraging communication and cooperation.

The book is designed to look at such practical concerns as: effective pain and symptom control; dying at home, in a hospice or in a hospital; patient/family/caregiver rights and responsibilities; ways to encourage open communication; and methods to improve overall cooperation.

I do not pretend to be an expert, so I have relied on the knowledge and advice of people who are experts in their respective fields. Except for personal interviews and written materials from numerous organizations, all the information in this book was found in sources listed in the Recommended Readings.

From my own personal experiences I believe that people need clear, brief and practical information. The majority of those actively involved with people who are dying do not have the time to read long, detailed or theoretical books. They want something that can help today. For those who want greater detail, or want to examine clinical studies or academic presentations I have included an annotated list of recommended readings.

My parents and grandfather all died within a five year period. They were not afraid of death as much as they were afraid of how they would die. In all three cases I was fortunate enough to be one of the people helping them to die at home. Had we known more about proper pain control techniques, hospice and homecare alternatives, patient and family rights, financial planning, etc., we could have provided even better care. We wanted to do so much more for the people we loved but we didn't know how. We didn't know where to get the information about how to provide better care.

Terminal illness does not mean a failure to cure. It does not mean that the disease has to rob us of our ability and need to love and to care. Terminal simply means "last" and in that sense of the word, a terminal illness is simply our last illness.

Personal control is all too often lost when a diagnosis of terminal illness is made. People who have been in charge of their careers, their homes and especially their own minds, find themselves powerless to direct their lives. Control comes from understanding what the options are and making decisions based upon reliable information. Knowledge decreases fear while increasing personal control.

Physicians, nurses and other caregivers are no strangers to the frustrations of terminal illness. Until recently, their education contained little information about terminal illness and ways to help their dying patients. These dedicated people were taught how to cure people, so to admit there is no cure goes against all of their professional training. They also feel a loss of control.

All of us have different experiences, religious and moral beliefs and ways of making decisions. Patients and families may decide to leave most of the decisions in the hands of their caregivers or they may choose to actively make their own decisions based on counsel from caregivers, other family members, and clerics. My concern is that people know they have options and that they can exercise control over their medical treatment.

Although the focus of this book is primarily on the patients understanding their options, I cannot deal with these issues without a great deal of empathy for the role of the family and caregivers in a patient's life. Often, final decisions about a person's life and death are left to these people. Their role is crucial and our understanding of how it affects us is very important to total patient care.

A few words about the structure and style of this book. I have collected all of the detailed anecdotes and placed them in Chapters Two, Four and Seven. I assume that many people will read only some of the chapters in this book, depending on their needs and available time. For those of you with limited time I assumed that you would want quick and practical information, so I have kept most of the chapters crisp and to the point. I have used various terms and expressions repeatedly throughout the book and although this might prove tiresome to those of you who read the entire book, I believe it is important to keep each chapter as a separate and complete unit.

I have tried to write in a style that reflects the importance of both women and men in the caregiving professions. If at times this style is awkward, I apologize, but there is, as yet, no universally acceptable style of writing that incorporates gender-neutral pronouns to replace "he" or "she."

Many of you reading this book are presently involved in a personal and/or professional way with someone who is dying. I encourage you to adapt the book to your personal or professional needs since I designed this book to meet the concerns and interests of as many different people as possible. For professionals in the field, I believe this book will be very useful to your patients as a basic understanding of what their choices are while encouraging them to work with you for improved total care.

I strongly believe that improving communication and cooperation will lead to comfort and peace for a person who is dying, and personal satisfaction for those who are helping people to live as fully as possible until they die. This is not an idealistic dream or a personal crusade but rather a goal that is reached every day by some people receiving proper pain and symptom control, emotional support and loving care.

CHAPTER ONE

UNDERSTANDING SOME OF THE BASICS

Patient/Family Relationships with Their Physician
Palliative/Hospice Care
Pain Control
Symptom Control
Legal and Moral Rights and Responsibilities
Euthanasia
Emotional Aspects of Death and Dying

Some people will pick up this book during an emergency and not have time to read each chapter thoroughly. The following general points should help you understand some of your choices. More detail is offered in each specific chapter. Use the Table of Contents to find the answers to your specific concerns.

This book is based on the assumption that we all have the individual right to choose how we cope with terminal illness. Some patients will choose to leave the major medical decisions to their caregivers. Others will want a more active role in directing their medical care. At all times, it is important to keep in mind the personal, financial and geographic limitations of the individual and the limitations of the medical system. The different things that patients, families and caregivers want are not always possible. This book suggests ways to provide medical and family supports to a person who is dying but the book is not meant to imply that this period of living until death is simple or without physical and emotional hardships.

PATIENT/FAMILY RELATIONSHIPS WITH PHYSICIAN

To encourage open communication and cooperation with your physicians I suggest:

1. Know your physicians' names and help them remember yours;
2. Write down important questions (generally not more than three at a time) and write down their answers;
3. Ask concise questions i.e., "What do you expect to find out by giving Dad these tests?" rather than "Why did this attack happen?";

4. Offer a time limit for discussion with your physician (about ten minutes) and stick to it. If your physician knows that you have specific questions that can be discussed in ten minutes she is more likely to spend the necessary time with you;
5. Speak openly about your concerns and fears and ask your physician if she can recommend someone else who can give practical information to you about what is happening, i.e. hospital social worker, specific books, nurse, health information organizations.

Alternative Therapies In emergency situations you will not have time to research and find alternative therapies for symptom relief or improved health. When you have time to examine some of the alternative therapies, check with your family physician, friends and relatives, consumer organizations and health information organizations to see what positive and negative effects such therapies have had on other people with a similar illness.

Alternative therapies are not a replacement for conventional medical care; they may be a supplement. A good family physician will help you coordinate conventional medicine with various alternative therapies.

PALLIATIVE/HOSPICE CARE

Palliative and Hospice care mean the same thing and I will be using the term hospice care. Hospice care is a philosophy of active and compassionate care of people with a terminal illness aimed at improving the quality of their remaining lives physically, emotionally and spiritually. A multidisciplinary approach, it brings together physicians, nurses, therapists, clerics, psychologists/psychiatrists and volunteers to work with the patients, families and the community.

PAIN CONTROL

Many terminal illnesses do not have overwhelming pain associated with them. According to physicians involved in hospice care, where there is pain, it is controllable in over 90% of the cases. The secret to effective pain control (relief) is giving the right drug, in the right amount, in the right way and at the right time. Proper pain medication prevents pain from returning while keeping the patient alert.

Pain control requires a special understanding of modern therapeutic techniques and many physicians (including cancer specialists) have not been adequately trained in this field. If a patient is suffering pain, the physician should be asked to refer the patient to a pain control specialist.

There are several myths about pain medication which are exactly that — myths. In fact, patients using narcotic pain medications (e.g. morphine) will not become addicted, they will not develop a tolerance, nor will they generally suffer from hallucinations as a result of taking drugs which have been properly administered. Pain medication should not be given as the patient begins to feel pain again. Some physicians prescribe drugs "as needed" which implies that the patient must begin to feel pain again before more medication is given. A proper medication schedule should prevent pain from returning at all.

SYMPTOM CONTROL

One of the most common causes of vomiting in cancer patients is constipation. Bed sores are painful and almost always preventable. These and other symptoms are controllable. They require special care and families are excellent caregivers in these areas if taught proper techniques.

LEGAL AND MORAL RIGHTS AND RESPONSIBILITIES

Legal rights have their source in laws. Moral rights have their source in generally accepted principles which may or may not be enforceable by law.

Some Basic Patient Legal Rights These include:
1. the right to consent or refuse any treatment as long as the consequences of this action are not harmful to others;
2. that consent must be based on a reasonable understanding of the nature, risks and alternatives to the treatment;
3. that consent to, or refusal of, treatment will be followed even if the patient later becomes incompetent;
4. the right to alter hospital/medical consent forms to conform to the patient's wishes. A physician or hospital may accept or refuse these revisions;
5. the right to choose or change physicians. The physician also has the right to choose his patients except in emergency situations;
6. the right not to take part in research or educational procedures.

Some Basic Caregiver Legal Rights Caregivers, especially physicians, are rightly given protection under the law for their medical judgment. For example, if, in a physician's opinion, a comatose patient requires life-support systems to give the physician an opportunity to improve the patient's health, then her opinion can overrule the family's expressed wishes on the patient's behalf.

In emergency situations when patients are unable to speak for themselves, emergency physicians and nurses have a responsibility to treat patients with or without the consent of their family. The law still assumes that in emergency situations physicians know what is best.

Most professions have a Code of Ethics which outlines their responsibilities to the patient and family.

Some Basic Family Legal Rights Generally speaking, the family cannot go against a patient's expressed wishes for or against a treatment. In fact, a primary purpose of this book is to stress our need to respect a patient's wishes. The greatest difficulties for family members arise when they wish to make decisions on behalf of loved ones who are unable to speak for themselves. Physicians should listen to a family's directives but they are not bound by them.

EUTHANASIA

Euthanasia refers to ending someone's life for compassionate reasons when a person is terminally ill or his suffering has become unbearable. Euthanasia can be passive (withdrawing life-support systems and treatment) or active (injection of a lethal dose of medication, assisted suicides). Suicide is legal in North America but helping someone to commit suicide, even if that person is incapable of committing suicide without help, is illegal and punishable by imprisonment. Active euthanasia (with or without the person's consent) is always illegal.

Withdrawing someone's life-support systems or treatment is sometimes permissible in circumstances where:
1. the patient refuses the treatment;
2. the patient is comatose and the physicians and family agree that life support systems and treatments are no longer helping the patient to improve or;
3. the patient is considered legally dead. It is also permissible under certain specific circumstances not to try to resuscitate a terminally ill patient who is near death and who has stopped breathing.

EMOTIONAL ASPECTS OF DEATH AND DYING

There are three groups of people affected when someone is dying: the person who is dying, family and friends, and caregivers. Individuals react in different ways and for different reasons but there are common feelings.

Two of the most important things to remember about how different people react to emotional difficulties are:
1. people's feelings of grief, anger, fear, joy, and frustration are real and should be talked about. The world does feel sometimes like it is coming apart but there are ways to deal with these feelings. The most recommended process for dealing with your feelings is by talking with family and friends and/or with professional people who regularly deal with these situations;

2. sometimes people say or do things that unintentionally hurt the person they care about. If their concern and caring are real then any errors they make are overshadowed by their compassion and love. There are specific things you can do to improve the life of someone who is dying, but few are greater than your expression of caring.

CHAPTER TWO

PERSONAL PERSPECTIVES

Chapters Two, Four and Seven represent the personal accounts of some of the people I interviewed for this book. These people have deep feelings about the treatment of patients who have a terminal illness and their families. They spoke with sensitivity and compassion without being sanctimonious. Their responses to questions were honest and unreserved. They are not missionaries in the cause of revolutionizing medical practices. They are people asking for improved coopera-tion and communication among caregivers and the people they treat. When you read their stories I think you will find that the caregivers place human compas-sion and concern above strict professional procedures. They are people first and caregivers second.

Rather than write their stories in a question-and-answer format I have de-cided, with their permission, to summarize their thoughts and write them as if they were speaking directly to you. Some of the people have asked that their real names and occupations not be used.

Never before in my years of researching have I left interviews with such a warm and reassured feeling. These people really care about who they are and how they can best help others. The handshakes or hugs that ended these inter-views put a broad smile on my face and a lighter step in my walk. I thank them for sharing their stories with all of us.

A DYING PERSON'S OWN STORY

"Like many veterans I am not afraid of death; I am afraid of how I die."

Hans Peters (not his real name) was a farm manager in his mid 50's. He was widowed a few years before his own death. This is his story compiled from several interviews. He had a lot he wanted to say to people. He wanted to help others understand what dying means so that people could benefit from his experiences.

I am dying but I am not afraid of death. I stopped being afraid of death that May morning in 1940 when I looked up from milking our family cow to see a Nazi soldier pointing a rifle at me. I fought later in another war and saw death all around me. Through my experiences I became more afraid of how I would die rather than death itself.

I won't live much longer now. My doctors tell me I have emphysema. It feels like a tight chain around my chest. You breathe and breathe and don't seem to get any air into your lungs. For the last few weeks I've been breathing oxygen from a tank. It makes my mouth dry and I can get "high" if I breathe too much of it. I've been smoking steady for 45 years now and this is the result, but what the hell — when I was a kid on the farm my father gave all his sons a pouch of tobacco on the day we graduated from elementary school. My wife kept telling me to stop smoking but it was too hard for me to do and I enjoyed it so much. When my wife died I smoked even more and cared about it less.

With emphysema you can live for many years, so they say. But I have a brain tumor too, which my physicians can't operate on so I will die pretty soon. One of the many doctors who looked after me was surprised that I didn't worry too much about death. She was a young neurologist and really upset by the news she had to give me about my illness, especially that I only have a few months to live. She hadn't experienced death as often as I had and was afraid of how I would react to her news.

After the initial shock wore off I took stock of my life and with few exceptions was quite pleased. I had married the girl of my dreams and our kids have grown to be good, hardworking and loving people.

You know I was a farmer. When the doctor found out I was a farmer, she told my kids that farmers understand death much better than other people. Farmers understand how seasons affect the life-cycle: in spring, life begins; in summer, life grows and becomes productive; while in the fall, life's work is harvested. Of course the winter season is that short period when life ends, only to begin again very soon in a new form. No big deal.

I believe in God and in an afterlife. When my wife was in a coma she saw heaven and said it was more beautiful, glorious and exciting than even our love for each other or the birth of our kids. She described her vision as her standing on one side of a flowing yet shallow river. She told me: "I had to make a choice of whether to cross the river or return to my family. It was the hardest choice I've ever made for heaven was so beautiful. I chose to come back here because I knew I couldn't leave you yet." She told me of the most peaceful world she had ever seen. I believed her then and I am comforted by the memory of her words now.

Death isn't scary for me anymore. How I die is what keeps bugging me. Some "ifs" about how and when I die are still scary. What worries me most, I suppose, is that my life was prolonged during my last hospital stay by some well-meaning people who didn't understand that I was ready to die. I hope it doesn't happen again. I want to die at home where I feel I have some control over what happens to me.

I saw my wife's life prolonged. Although we took her home and gave her what pain medication we had, the pain she suffered was unnecessary and humiliating for such a strong-minded and loving woman. It broke my heart to watch her, knowing I was quite helpless to make her death more dignified.

I also worry about my three grown-up kids. I don't want to put them through another period of caring for a dying parent. They don't complain and even gained strength through their mother's death but I still feel it is unfair to them and unfair to me. I am their father who helped raise them. They should not have to see me die away in a slow process of hospitalization, new medications to combat side-effects of other medications (I am taking over 15 kinds of drugs right now), or my body losing weight so that I look like a concentration camp victim.

Hell, I deserve better. Everyone deserves better. I'm angry sometimes at the injustice that we humans put each other through. On a farm, when an animal is ill beyond hope, we mercifully let it die with some dignity. Yet we civilized human beings cannot agree on a system so that people can die as they deserve. We are afraid of death so we prolong our lives to avoid dying.

I do deserve better than this. My kids deserve better than this and when you think about it, the doctors and nurses taking care of me deserve better than this. My death shouldn't be dependent on medicine or technology alone; it should also be my decision. But even these people, who deal with death every day, don't know how to handle it. How then should other people: family, friends, our employers or colleagues know how to cope?

Perhaps one of the hardest things I've gone through is the way I was treated at work. I left our family farm in the 1940s and ended up years later working as a farm manager for a relatively small farming company. I worked for over ten years to help make that business profitable and was rewarded every year with a raise in salary. The owner was still pretty young when I started and I thought over the years that we had become friends, not just an employer and employee. We had our professional arguments but they never lasted long.

Things began to change when I started to slow down a bit at work. One day I couldn't breathe well and was rushed to hospital. My kids were scared to death but I came out of it pretty well. I didn't know yet how serious my illness would become and chalked it up to exertion and stress.

My boss came to visit me during that first hospital stay and told me how much I was missed at the office and that I shouldn't worry about my work until I had a good rest. I needed my work and he knew that. His words were very comforting.

While getting better at home a few weeks later, I had what my kids thought was a stroke. I was rushed to hospital where the doctors decided I had had a seizure, not a stroke. Drugs controlled my seizures but my emphysema had also worsened enough so that I had to begin using a portable oxygen tank.

After this latest hospital stay my boss visited me again and told me I had to retire for the good of the company. I was stunned, hurt, furious and disappointed all at the same time. I was trying to get my physical and emotional health back into shape so I didn't need to find out that I had lost my financial security as well.

All of this happened before I found out about my brain tumor and that I probably only had a few months to live. Normally emphysema patients can live up to five years after they go on permanent oxygen use. I thought I would have a few more years where I could be productive at work and maybe play with some grandkids as well. I am still in my 50s after all. I felt betrayed by my body and needed the support of my job more than ever.

I knew it was difficult for my boss to deal with my illness. It would have been so much easier for us to talk openly about our feelings and fears. He has a business to run but I think I could have helped him in return for his continued trust and respect. At first I blamed him for forcing my retirement but then I tried to imagine how people must feel when they find out that someone they have worked with for years is very ill. I don't think he knew how to cope with my illness and figured it was best for both of us if we parted company. Illness, as with any handicap, doesn't rob us of our abilities; well-meaning but unaware people do.

What would I suggest to other employers under similar circumstances? Terminal illness does not mean that a person is useless. It means so much for people to feel useful and needed. Employers and employees need to realize that working together can be mutually beneficial.

Now that I know I am dying I have a few suggestions for my friends as well. It is very important to me that they accept the fact that I am dying. It doesn't help me to hear them say that I am looking better or that I will be up and about soon. I won't. When some of my friends do not accept that I am dying it makes it difficult for me to talk about what I feel and what my hopes are for them. By their actions, they are saying they don't want to hear or face the reality of my death; nor I guess their own death.

When some people are unable to talk openly, it also makes it difficult for my kids because they have fewer people to lean on. Fortunately, I have family and friends who do accept the natural process of my dying. It is their gift to my kids and me that can never be repaid.

What about my medical treatment? Doctors and other medical staff often mean well but they sometimes forget they are dealing with people. When things first began happening to me it was all too fast for me to think clearly. My kids were very worried and therefore they took over asking the questions that needed to be asked, for example, "What is happening?" "How soon can he come home?" "Is there anything we can do?" "What are his chances of recovery?" "What things do you think we need to know to help us to help him?" Often these questions were dodged because there were no clear answers. There were educated guesses, however, and I think we deserved to know what they were.

I was brought into emergency five times before coming home to die and in three of those times I was given too much oxygen which made me "drunk" for days. I don't remember my son's birthday because I was "out of it" for three days. The frustrating thing for my family was that the first two times it happened, no one believed my kids when they told doctors that I wasn't acting as I normally would. They said my kids were exaggerating what they saw and were being too protective of me.

When my kids finally got the doctor to explain why I had appeared intoxicated or senile for a few days at a time they were able to protect me from it recurring the next time I was rushed to the hospital. In other words, when they were made aware of the facts, or educated guesses, of what was happening to me they could work together with the medical staff to give me the best care I could get.

So often in the hospital I heard other patients complain that people weren't listening to them. It seems to me life would be easier if everyone worked together, for it would spread the knowledge around to the people who know the patient best and who can assist him the best. Nurses often complained of the same thing. They admitted the doctors were extremely busy and therefore only had five-to-ten minutes to spend with each patient. What infuriated them was that they were the professional staff who saw the patients the most, yet their opinion was often not even consulted, never mind listened to.

People make life so complicated when really it is quite simple. Imagine all the lawsuits that would never be laid against doctors, nurses, and hospitals if the patients and their families were involved from the beginning. A simple consent form isn't enough. Knowledge gives me self-confidence and some form of control which after nearly 60 years of living I have gotten used to having.

Perhaps one day, writers and the rest of the world will talk more with people who are dying. Better yet, let's get the children and the politicians to talk to us. They could learn a lot about living from people who are dying.

There are three things that keep coming back to me these days and maybe you can use them for your book. It will be the last time I guess that anything I say will mean something to more than just my kids and friends.

Faith in God makes accepting death easier. Faith in people will give people, like me, a more dignified death in the future than is possible today.

Employers need to understand that one day they will die as well and therefore they should benefit from the presence of someone who may be dying but hasn't given up on life or given up on being productive.

Friends need to understand as well that dying people still have the normal needs that we all have. I still think of having a good time, playing cards, reading the newspaper, getting into a good political argument. I enjoy laughing even though at times I need to cry. If my wife were alive, I would still enjoy sex and the comfort of a kiss and a hug. I also need to talk about my death which is not meant to be morbid or to remind you that you are going to die one day too. Dying is not scary all the time but sometimes I feel I have to handle it all by myself because people don't understand what it's like.

My kids have been super for they hug me and let me hug back, they talk about how they feel and about how I feel, they help me make plans and try to insure that I get the best treatment available. Sometimes they love me too much and that makes me sad because I know I must leave them. That is the hardest of all.

My wish is that my life has had a positive impact on my family and friends and also on people who have met me briefly: during the war, with my community work or just because I happened to smile at a stranger one day not knowing that he, too, may have lost a dear friend recently.

I also hope that when it is time for me to go I can say goodbye with some dignity to encourage my kids to build their strengths and their love. How we part company will be in their memories for the rest of their lives and I hope I will be able to make it loving and special, for they deserve at least that much.

Hans died with his children beside him. His death at home was not beautiful, nor dignified, as he had hoped. However his children did grow stronger and their love did increase. They are very proud of their parents, just as their father and mother were proud of them. They hope to write a family history one day, so that their children can learn from the grandparents they will never know.

CHAPTER THREE

PATIENT/FAMILY RELATIONSHIPS WITH THEIR PHYSICIAN

Understanding the Physician
Understanding Patients and Their Families
What Physicians Can Learn from Their Patients
Some Do's and Don'ts of Improved Communication
Resolving Communication Problems
Family Meetings
Alternative Therapies

This book concentrates on how people can work together for the improved total care of someone who has a terminal illness. A key relationship during this period is the one between the patient/family and their various physicians. While this chapter concentrates on this relationship, many of the points are also applicable to relationships patients and families have with other caregivers. Mutual respect and open communication are just as important with nurses, clerics, therapists, and other caregivers as with a physician.

The medical world is going through a rapid and tremendous change. There are increased pressures on caregivers including the added responsibilities to other medical personnel, intervention by governments and insurance bodies, limitations on payment for consultations, phone advice and sometimes the type of service caregivers are permitted to give. The increased demands by consumer organizations compared to the relatively slow adaptability of the medical system causes even further tension.

The result of this rapidly changing system requires everyone to recognize the financial and resource limitations during this time when a patient is dying. Limited hospice programs, medical services, and caregiver time all affect the kind of care a patient can expect. Understanding these limitations will help people to have realistic expectations of the type of care available to them while also encouraging them to find ways to adapt to the specific limitations of their case.

There is a natural apprehension by the patient and family toward physicians. Most of them are afraid of their illness but they must rely on the expertise and advice of a person they may not know. In the past few years, there has been a heightened awareness that when the patient/family work together with their physician everyone benefits. Open and honest communication relieves the patient and family's anxiety, while the physicians feel more job satisfaction and less personal stress.

UNDERSTANDING THE PHYSICIAN

Caregivers endure stresses that everyone can help diminish by working together. The professional stresses of a physician include:

1. heavy workload (it isn't enough to be a physician these days; you must also be a business person, a politician, and a bureaucrat);
2. deciding how much patients should know about their serious illness (although most patients prefer to know the truth about their illness, there are patients who prefer that the physician not tell them the complete truth);
3. the increasing administrative requirements of governments and insurance companies;
4. little time to learn new treatments and methods;
5. little time for personal stress reduction;
6. increasing numbers of lawsuits; and
7. a decreased public respect for the medical profession in general.

A common complaint against physicians is that they are uncommunicative. Dr. Peter Hanson, the author of *The Joy of Stress,* explains why some physicians may appear uncommunicative. Physicians, especially specialists, have often gone directly from high school, to university, then to medical school, and finally specialty training. They have limited experience or training in communication skills with people outside the medical community, especially people from different cultural and economic backgrounds.

Many graduates from medical schools have either a domineering, paternalistic personality or an analytic, detail-oriented personality. These personality types can make communication difficult. Some of these physicians are basically quite shy and do not realize that they are being uncommunicative. With diplomacy and persistence patients and families can help physicians become more communicative even in today's chaotic, rapidly changing medical system.

Many physicians are uncomfortable with patients who are dying. After all, medical training is designed to cure patients not help them to die. Medical training has indirectly seen death as a failure of modern medicine. Dealing with the emotional stresses of patients dying is not part of most medical training. Medical ethics about life and death decisions are only now being offered in some medical schools. If physicians are uncomfortable about speaking of death and dying they should tell their patients. Patients may be able to help their physicians understand what it is like to be dying. At the same time, patients can feel useful by helping their doctors.

Some eminent physicians have written on the subject of physician-patient relationships. Sir William Osler, 19th-century Canadian physician, diagnostician and scholar, began the Internal Medicine department at Johns Hopkins Hospital, helped begin the Rockefeller Foundation and taught students like the Mayo brothers (of Mayo clinic fame). Sir William believed that it is more important to know what type of patient has a disease rather than what type of disease a patient has. He gave his patients little medication but lots of optimism. That optimism is just as important to someone who is dying but takes the form of encouraging a full life until one dies.

Norman Cousins in his book *The Anatomy of an Illness* describes a visit he had with Dr. Albert Schweitzer in Africa. Schweitzer explained his philosophy of medical practice. He believed that each person carries his own doctor inside of him. He goes to a physician because he does not recognize his own strength. A physician's greatest asset is his ability to bring out the doctor within his patients. By helping patients gain a sense of personal control over their lives, physicians are also achieving a professional satisfaction that they are making a positive difference in the lives of their patients.

UNDERSTANDING PATIENTS AND THEIR FAMILIES

Quality total care looks at the physical, emotional and spiritual needs of the patient. Studies show that people who have a terminal illness want many of the same things including:
1. to be pain free;
2. to be alert and aware of what is happening to them;
3. to have the companionship of their family and friends;
4. to be accepted as the person they have always been;
5. to maintain their individuality;
6. not to die alone (this is especially true in cases where people, most often women, have already lost their spouse);
7. not to be a burden to their family and caregivers;
8. to have familiar things around them: photos, plants, music, flowers, favorite food, pets;
9. to be cared for and remembered with love and respect; and
10. to have their family continue living and loving after their death.

Patients and familes must accept responsibility for encouraging improved communication with their physician because the consequences of an uncooperative relationship affects the patient and family most directly. This is not always easy because some people have a real fear of anything medical. Other barriers to effective communication can include family tensions, lack of anyone nearby for support, and lack of services for our rapidly aging population.

There are, quite naturally, patients who have a difficult time adjusting to the constraints of a terminal illness. They may fight their illness or completely submit to it. They may communicate very little with their families or not cooperate with their caregivers. These are difficult times for everyone involved and it requires a continued effort by family and caregivers to meet the individual needs of the patient. People need a sense of control that comes only from making decisions, even if they are considered wrong. You cannot force patients to agree to all the changes going on in their lives, nor can you stand by as if the consequences of their decisions do not affect you personally. Patients need to be told what the consequences of their actions are and how they affect the family and other caregivers. Sometimes the situation will improve for everyone concerned but, realistically speaking, some people will never communicate or cooperate.

WHAT PHYSICIANS CAN LEARN FROM THEIR PATIENTS

There are many things physicians can learn from their patients, especially those who are dying, and from the families. Professional development programs will also help physicians become more comfortable with their patients' deaths as well as their own deaths.

Things that physicians can learn from their patients include:
1. facts about their condition (This seems obvious but some symptoms are not adequately addressed by the physician because the patient does not talk about new symptoms, there are time constraints or the physician or patient makes presumptions about the condition);
2. new treatments that patients have read about in a popular magazine or seen on a television program that the physician has not investigated. Admittedly, some of these treatments are not proven but discussing them with patients will get them more actively involved in their treatment. That sense of control improves a patient's self-image and decreases anxiety.
3. patients are the constant factor over the months or years of treatment. They were there for every pain, symptom, test and operation. They can offer vital feedback on their present treatments, feelings and fears;
4. patients, with the physician's encouragement, can express their needs and therefore help the physician in determining further treatment.

SOME DO'S AND DON'TS OF IMPROVED COMMUNICATION

From the physician and other caregivers' points of view there are proven techniques that patients can use to improve the patient-caregiver relationship.

Some Do's:
1. know their caregivers' names and help them remember theirs;
2. communicate with them about their physical and emotional needs and feelings;
3. cooperate fully once a decision on treatment is mutually decided;
4. write down the important questions to ask (usually in groups of three) and record the caregiver's answers;
5. respect the caregiver's time while expecting the same in return;

6. ask precisely answerable questions rather than "Why did this happen to me?";
7. offer a time limit for discussion (e.g. 5 minutes) and stick to it. In this way you build up a trusting relationship with the caregivers and they know you respect their time.

Some Don'ts: Some patients will choose not to follow the following suggestions and, in effect, choose not to communicate and cooperate. Whether we agree with their decision or not, it is their decision and they must be respected (unless they injure someone else).

1. **Don't** ignore medical instructions after a mutual medical decision has been made;
2. **Don't** ask too many questions, over and over again, (it is best to make notes of the physician's answers);
3. **Don't** bring up questions about other family members and friends in hope of free medical advice;
4. **Don't** keep telephoning with questions that can be better answered by other experts such as a nurse, pharmacist or therapist;
5. **Don't** wait to communicate new pains or negative symptoms until they have become serious;
6. **Don't** forget to communicate emotional needs, (often patients just show a brave face to their physicians);
7. **Don't** get a second medical opinion without first telling the principal physician, (consider the extra financial burdens involved in getting a second opinion);
8. **Don't** follow other medical or alternative therapies without consulting the principal physician because the different therapies may conflict; and don't forget to treat the caregivers with respect or concern.

RESOLVING COMMUNICATION PROBLEMS

When open communication does not seem possible, there are other options available. When the problem has become serious, bring in the hospital, hospice or community social worker to see if improvements can be made. Other caregivers such as a cleric, nurse, or psychologist may also be helpful.

Where the communication cannot be improved, the patient/family can do one or both of the following (although I recognize that during such an emotional time these suggestions will not be easy to follow):

1. change specialists on the advice of your family physician or another caregiver;
2. change hospitals or the service you are using.

If it is the patient or family that is uncooperative, the physician might recommend a different physician or hospital. She must legally continue care until the patient has found a new physician.

Many communication problems are not always one person's fault. People have different personalities and for whatever reason, some people do not communicate well with each other. If both people recognize the problem and accept the situation, the caregiver can help find someone to replace him.

In the case of family members, a physician may find it easier to speak to a single member of the family rather than the whole family. Recognizing that the patient is the physician's paramount concern, the family can arrange to choose a member to act as spokesperson and minimize the time a physician needs to spend with the whole family.

FAMILY MEETINGS

A family member or the responsible physician can organize a family meeting or conference to help clarify the options and needs of the patient and family.

This special time helps a family stop and think about what they are going through, what the patient is going through and how, by working as a team, everyone's needs can best be met.

The specific goals of the meeting are presented, along with ideas on how the family, friends and caregivers can work most effectively together. Each person can bring up those specific things they can contribute, i.e. housekeeping, babysitting, cooking, spending time with the person dying, or perhaps driving people to do shopping or visiting.

The meeting should also permit people to say what they do not want to do, i.e. bathe the patient, talk to caregivers or give medications.

The meetings can be regular and should provide all participants with support and encouragement. These gatherings should also permit people to discuss communication or patient-care problems. Above all, when approached from a positive perspective, problems can be solved and acceptable compromises can be arrived at.

ALTERNATIVE THERAPIES

I have included alternative therapies in this chapter because I feel that family physicians must coordinate the overall medical treatment of their patients. Therefore, patients should consult their physicians before trying any new therapies. If the patient wants to try a therapy, the physician can suggest resources which present both the pros and cons. In cases where the family physician does not believe in any form of alternative therapy, the patient can research the therapy through a library, medical reports or organizations listed in the appendix. Regardless of the physician's opinion, it is important that patients inform their physicians about any therapies they are trying.

The increase in alternative health organizations and treatments force us to be more careful in choosing what is appropriate for us. Some family physicians may encourage their patients to try various other treatments not offered by them as long as:

    a. the treatment is not harmful;

    b. is not expensive (most fraudulent therapies are very expensive);

    c. the practitioners can prove their claims; and

    d. the practitioners encourage continued communication with the family physicians.

There are holistic physicians, nurses, therapists and others who have received traditional medical training. There are also those without a medical background who have taken certified training from a recognized training facility. There are other practitioners who can prove neither their qualifications nor their results.

The decision to try an alternative therapy is a personal one and should be made in consultation with your physician and other people you trust. Take precautions to ensure that you are dealing with committed and knowledgeable practitioners. I have included a list of organizations at the back of this book where you can call or write for more detailed information.

There are as many forms of alternative therapies as there are people willing to develop them. Some of these therapies result in physical and/or emotional improvements while others remain in the area of consumer fraud.

Holistic health is a system of medical care that emphasizes the whole person: physical, nutritional, environmental, emotional, spiritual and lifestyle. While it encompasses all safe methods of diagnosis and treatment including surgery and medications when appropriate, the difference between holistic and traditional medical care is that patients take a more active role in their own care. Part of this holistic philosophy includes:

1. maintaining a positive attitude toward living to the fullest with hope, humor and inner calm;
2. reducing environmental and emotional stresses through relaxation exercises and recreational activities;
3. encouraging positive stresses through challenge, nature walks, sex, art and music appreciation;
4. eating nutritiously;
5. having caring relationships with others and providing support to others;
6. using prayer, meditation, visualization and imaging to optimize prevention and healing;
7. seeking professional advice and counseling when needed.

I cannot go into detail here about all the alternative treatments available but I will list a few of the more commonly known ones. Many of these therapies are still not accepted by traditional medical people and remain controversial. I am not qualified to suggest that people try or avoid these therapies. There are many medical reports that support or oppose the use of these therapies. Most of the therapies are not included in medical insurance benefits so it is very important to consider the financial costs.

The decision to try alternative therapies must remain with patients. Families and physicians can provide information both pro and con for a particular therapy but they must respect the patient's decisions unless such decisions will lead to harmful, expensive therapies. True holistic therapies are neither harmful nor very expensive.

Acupuncture An ancient Chinese technique where sterile needles are inserted through the skin in pre-determined points, often remote from the site of the actual disorder or pain. A primary modern usage is to reduce pain.

Autosuggestion Also called autogenic training or self-hypnotism, autosuggestion is a methodical system of meditative exercises and deep relaxation, formulated on the principle that the body will naturally balance itself when directed into a relaxed state. Proven useful in treating ulcers, constipation, blood pressure, migraines, asthma, diabetes, arthritis, and pain, it is also becoming more popular as a stress management technique.

Biofeedback A self-directed relaxation technique to help regulate your own pulse rate, body temperature and muscle tension. It has, therefore, been effective for people with: high blood pressure, migraine headaches, muscle spasms, back and neck pain, and general tension. Like all relaxation techniques, biofeedback is useful in managing stress, fear or anxiety.

Chiropractic Care A philosophy, science and art to correct interference in the nervous system with the spinal column as the life-line of the system. Chiropractors manipulate the spine to return its vertebrae to a balanced state, thereby easing back and neck stress and pain. Practitioners also include preventive exercises and improved-posture, nutrition and lifestyle programs to maintain a balanced system.

Herbal Therapy Based on Native American, Chinese and Eastern peoples' methods, herbalism has been used to supply vitamins and minerals the body needs without the danger of toxic side effects.

Naturopathy Seeks to balance the relationship between the mind, body and spirt of the individual and his environment, in nature. Naturopathy attempts to improve the resistance within the body to the disease through nourishing the body with natural foods and water in order to cleanse the body of its toxins. Emphasis is also placed on developing peace of mind through relaxation exercises, visualizations and meditation.

Osteopathy A medical therapy that emphasizes manipulative techniques for correcting body ailments believed to be caused by the pressure of displaced bones on nerves.

Therapeutic Touch A simple, ancient method of healing based on the principle of laying-on-of-hands using the energy in one person's hands to help balance the energy in someone else's body. The modern version, taught in some American universities to student nurses, relies less on actually touching a patient but rather passing one's hands near the patient's body.

CHAPTER FOUR

CARING: TWO PERSPECTIVES

A Family Physician's Point of View
A Parent's Story of Caring for a Seriously-Ill Child

A FAMILY PHYSICIAN'S POINT OF VIEW

Dr. Carol Brock is a family physician who has taught family practice to physicians at a community hospital. I met Dr. Brock at her home where our short interview turned into a two and one-half hour discussion of the physician-patient relationship.

We began talking in her warmly-decorated living room about our mutual interest in old pine furniture. She has a beautiful antique wooden physician's desk, with dozens of little cubbyholes, used years ago for medicine bottles. It seemed appropriate that we were going to talk about how to encourage a cooperative and open relationship between family physicians and their patients near this old desk. There are many idealistic pictures we have of old country physicians and some of those ideals may be returning to modern family practice.

It was clear from the beginning that Dr. Brock had a sensitivity to the needs of her patients. Her choice of family practice was based more on her personal philosophy of what a family physician should be than what she had been taught about medicine during her professional training. The following is a summary of what Dr. Brock felt were the most important things to pass along to other family physicians, their patients and patients' families.

The most important role of family physicians, when one of their patients is dying, is to pay attention — not just to their words, for words often say what patients think they should say, but also to their body language. Looking into their eyes can help physicians understand their patients' fears and needs. Each situation is unique. For example, a patient or family member may come asking for your medical advice, when what she really needs is to have her hand held and told that her fears are natural and surmountable.

People will come to you at different times during the period when they or a loved one is dying. They come very soon after learning about their terminal illness from a specialist. They come during the living process leading to death and their family members will come to you after the person has died. What they often need most is someone who knows them well, will listen unconditionally and will explain in clear language the medical process of the illness and what they can expect to happen.

Although the listening and counselling is crucial to patient care, there are also the practical components to medical care that the family practitioner can help with. In effect, the family practitioner should be the patient's advocate with all the other members of the medical world: the hospital, specialists, social workers, homecare personnel and even the clergy when that appears appropriate.

Assuming there are family members and/or friends available to help the patient you can talk to the them in a family conference and help them make group decisions. A family conference permits people to volunteer how they can help the patient best: housekeeping, driving people to and from the hospital or appointments, or acting as the single family spokesperson with the medical specialists. During a family conference each family member can also talk about what he or she finds difficult to do: bathing the patient, talking about death and dying, or answering phone calls from other family and friends who want to know about the patient's condition.

In effect, the family phyisician is helping the family to stop for a few moments during a very traumatic time and review the various options available to them and consider what decisions must be made. This is naturally an ongoing process but once the family begins to work together (if this is possible), then the physician's time commitment does not have to be as great. As a family practitioner you can also suggest that your patients turn to the people closest to them for emotional, spiritual and physical support. It may appear obvious that people do this on their own, but so often people find it difficult to decide honestly what they really need in the way of support. People do not want to be a burden to someone else.

As a family practitioner, you can suggest that your patients relax in a comfortable chair, in a quiet place and think about what they really need in a physical, emotional and spiritual way. You can repeat often to your patients that once they have decided what they need, they must force themselves to ask for help. When people lived in smaller communities it wasn't as necessary to ask for help because people naturally helped each other. In today's urban world, we feel uncertain and are afraid to ask for help and our family and friends often feel they would be interfering if they offered their help.

If patients ask for help, but the person they ask cannot cope with the terminal illness, the patients should ask someone else. If the first few people asked are not able to give the patients the support they need, they should persist and ask someone else. I realize this is easier said than done but patients need support and family practitioners can help them get it.

Physicians or friends who say "There's nothing left to do," are doing a great disservice to the person. You have to help him find hope, and a way to cope, when all appears hopeless. There is always something you can do even if a cure is no longer one of the options. People can live a full life until their death, if they are given physical and emotional support.

People who are dying can put their financial and legal matters in order to save their survivors a great deal of frustration. They can also spend valuable time with their families and friends talking about future hopes and reminiscing about happy times in the past.

Families and friends can provide physical and emotional support by supplying prepared foods or baby-sitting. Being there yourself and being yourself is the most important thing you can do. Words are often not as important as listening, holding a hand, sharing a tear and saying, "I love you." A simple open-ended question like "How are you really feeling?" will permit the person who is dying or grieving to say as much or as little as she wishes.

One of the hardest things family and friends are asked to do is to listen repeatedly to someone who is grieving. It may appear that the person is living in the past yet, it is a common response to grief and sorrow and repetition makes the past and the death real and the healing effective.

Patients afraid of dying may ask their physicians very difficult questions, such as, what are God's reasons for their dying now, what are the physician's own beliefs regarding euthanasia, what will happen to their families, will they die in pain and will they die alone. Most often people will want an honest answer from their physician, not a church sermon remembered from the physician's childhood days. If you, as a physician, believe in an after-life, speak honestly about your belief. If you disagree with euthanasia in all cases, explain why. With the families, the physician can discuss how survivors of other patients dealt with the death of a loved one. Fears about pain are real but modern pain and symptom control techniques can take that pain away while keeping a person mentally alert. If you are unable to explain or prescribe adequate pain control, refer the patient to a physician who specializes in this field.

Patients are often afraid of dying alone but they may not talk about this fear. People, generally, do not want to be a burden to others. Reassure patients that you or a colleague are available to help at any time (patients don't usually abuse this offer) and discuss with the family ways to ensure that the person is never alone during the final period before death.

As a family practitioner I often see situations where there is little, unified family support. Part of the family wants one thing for the patient and another part wants something totally different. These are difficult situations at best and again the physician's primary concern is the patient's needs and desires. If it is possible, get the patient to designate a spokesperson for himself and encourage the family to concentrate on the patient's wishes rather than their own. If the situation is more difficult, try and bring other people into the picture who might help, such as a cleric, a social worker, or a support group/agency like the Cancer Society, a Bereaved Parents group etc.

Choices made by a patient, family and physician about treatment and medications are not always the right ones. It takes time and coordinated effort to find the right combination of medication and treatment for each patient's individual needs. If everyone works together as a team then the right choices are found more quickly. As a family physician, I believe everyone does his or her best at this time and if you come to the death of a loved one feeling you've done what you could and that I, as your family physician, have helped, then the death is an easier thing to accept for all concerned.

When I taught family practice to general practitioners I noticed, at first, an unconscious narrowness of mind when dealing with patient's emotional needs. This is not a condemnation but rather an observation. Many physicians are chosen by medical schools for their academic excellence rather than their interpersonal communication skills and aptitude for working with people.

Physicians are given little training in listening and communication skills. They have gone from high school to university and then medical school without a great deal of experience with the people they will serve. It is a situation that is slowly changing for the better. I am optimistic that improved physician-patient communication will lead to people having even more dignified lives until they die. This ideal situation is within our reach right now.

A personal note. I have changed my own personal ways of dealing with death and dying. I have learned many valuable lessons of living from my patients who were dying. I have also gone through a soul search to examine how my role as physician must sometimes change from that of curing patients to helping patients work with the choices available to them here and now. Personal friends, patients and reading books in various fields, including life-after-death issues, have helped me to understand even more clearly that there is still loving, giving and productivity when patients live until their death.

A PARENT'S STORY OF CARING FOR A SERIOUSLY-ILL CHILD

Often when we hear about terminal illness we see death as the worst possible situation. We think of the times we will miss, the special joys we cannot have together with someone, or the horrible waste of losing someone so special to us.

The following story I hope will help those who have, or will have, to face the difficult decisions that arise when parents have a seriously-ill baby. Depending on whom you ask you will find that there are things worse than dying. Living in constant pain, being unable to communicate or being unproductive are becoming indicators of "the quality of life." We can learn from the story of Jane and John Rogers. What they have experienced, and the hopes they have for their son, are lessons in understanding what may be worse than death, and also how people adapt their lives for someone they love. You will see quite clearly the love these parents have for their child but also the questions left unanswered when Ricky was so ill.

Jane and John Rogers and their two-year-old son Ricky (not their real names) live in a mid-sized city. Before her pregnancy Jane worked as a medical technologist. John commutes every day to another city where he is a stock broker. Ricky was born after a picture perfect pregnancy. His mother had no irregularities during her preg-

nancy and she was very conscious of her family's health. Ricky was two weeks overdue but his birth went well and he weighed in at 9 pounds 15 ounces. There were no indications that there was anything wrong. Here is Jane's story of what happened.

They took Ricky from the operating room and we thought everything was fine until my parents said that he had been placed in an incubator. He was a large baby, so the need for an incubator was disturbing. The nurse told my parents that it was common practice for babies to be put in incubators after they had been washed so that they would dry off safely.

Within short order Ricky had respiratory distress and the doctors found congestive heart failure. An ultrasound scan the next day showed a malformation of blood vessels in Ricky's brain and it was decided by the medical staff to transfer him to the Childrens' Hospital. Needless to say, we were very worried for I had to stay in my hospital a bit longer while John checked in on both of us.

After several weeks of tests and treatments we were suddenly told to take Ricky home. We were ecstatic but totally unprepared. No one was clear about what lay ahead. Opinions varied but included the possibility of our finding our son dead in his crib within a month, to having him stablized with medication for an indefinite period of time. Our questions were often unanswered, but as Ricky was able to come home we took full advantage of the time we would have together and thought things were going well. We even managed to deal with all the medications, scheduling and ridiculous numbers of doctors' appointments.

Ricky laughed, enjoyed playing and looking at everything and anything. His baby pictures are adorable if I say so myself. What parent wouldn't? About four months later we thought that Ricky's progress was slowing down compared to other children. By eight months, he was receiving occupational therapy and it became apparent that the malformation of his brain blood vessels would have to be treated in some way, probably with an operation.

With no choice but to trust the the neurosurgeon we placed our son in his care. We were not told enough about the probable consequences of the surgery should Ricky survive but felt good that the surgeon was positive about what improvements were possible.

It was an eleven-hour operation. We later discovered that only two other children with Ricky's diagnosis had ever survived. The surgeon's prognosis was very positive and he left for a conference. Within a short time Ricky began to have severe seizures and he was rushed to the Intensive Care Unit (ICU). He was given heavy medication but he still had bad seizures for two weeks. He was in a drug-induced coma for weeks longer. Everyone was extremely surprised that he pulled through all of these seizures, respirators, drugs and treatments, and woke up, breathing on his own. He was later diagnosed as being blind, unable to hear or communicate, quadriplegic, and having no real contact with the world.

There were many crises during that month including swelling of the brain, unsuccessful attempts to get him off the respirator, use of incorrect drugs, and the list goes on. Our saving grace was that the ICU doctors and nurses were always there and after a time began to listen to what we observed about Ricky's condition. They answered our questions as best they could.

All the parents got to know the ICU system and how to adapt it to their own child's best interests. We protected Ricky from too many blood tests when one test was sufficient. We stopped unnecessary procedures because we were the only caregiver there all the time and could then best help direct his care.

However, these little victories against modern medical treatment didn't negate the horrible sense of helplessness that we parents in ICU shared with each other. We banded together to protect ourselves from the often illogical system that was controlling our children's lives. It would have been invaluable to have a list of people within the hospital who could help us rather than being continually confronted by well-meaning social workers and other staff. They didn't understand that we needed to feel control over our own lives and the life of our son. The opportunity to choose our own support system, in peace, would have made a difference.

You can deal with death, with grief, with changing your whole life around, but you cannot deal with the frustration of losing control; of not having the information you need, or the team effort required to help a seriously-ill child.

It was amazing to see how some parents adapted to the stress and frustration. One teenage single parent from the eastern U.S. had very little education, yet she became an expert in medications. Her child had spina bifida which required seven operations. The child had spell after spell that the staff referred to as seizures and different medications didn't help. She checked with other parents there and finally asked her doctor why her son was not getting phenobarbital like other children. He listened to her (a gift, believe me), tried the drug and it worked. She was able to take her son home sooner than anyone had anticipated.

Many of the doctors we dealt with were uncomfortable with how Ricky was progressing and therefore ignored and avoided us. There was one physician, however, who did exactly what I suggest all doctors should do. He listened to our concerns and questions and when he didn't have a good answer he simply told the truth and suggested we look up some of the books in his office for an answer. His answers were always honest rather than technical or vague.

When Ricky did come out of the coma, and was stable, he was moved to a general ward. This was the worst experience of my life. You could hear children crying in fear or pain at all hours. It was so sad and painful and yet it is somewhat ironic that some children were at least well enough to cry. Our Ricky was not; he cannot cry.

In ICU, doctors and nurses are always there. On the wards, doctors are rarely seen and nurses are too overworked and overstressed to spend time with their patients and their families. Nurses get yelled at by doctors, by patients and by patients' families so the ones that are a source of comfort and information are a treasure.

John and I had to be there to make sure that medications were given on time and correctly. Sad to say if we were not there this would not have happened. Nutritional care was rigid in the hospital and we had to be sure food was given correctly. I fought with one nutritionist who said that a boy Ricky's age needed a tremendous number of calories per day. She did not take into account that he was completely inactive and therefore getting too many calories which would make him even more ill.

On wards, we were lied to by a doctor who didn't think we knew anything about medical treatments, even after I told him I worked as a medical technologist. One nurse was quite rude and patronizing because I insisted that Ricky be given medication on time. If these people had only let us, we could have lightened their workloads while also helping our son. We could have worked as a team with some mutual satisfaction at the end of each day.

John and I were under considerable stress during these months. If our marriage had not been strong we might not have survived. As it was, we grew stronger together and received great support from family and friends. One couple called to "kidnap" us for an hour. We left word at the hospital where we would be and went with them down the street for a meal away from the hospital. Other friends brought over casseroles for us to heat up in the microwave at the snackbar so we could have a home-cooked meal. These thoughtful gifts did much for our sanity and good health!

One thing we did not have time for was doing research on Ricky's disease. I am used to researching diseases and medical treatments but I couldn't bear to read about all the terrible possibilities that lay ahead for Ricky. What would have been very helpful was a list of support groups with people who had gone through similar situations. We felt so alone at times; so isolated.

In some of the reading I did before Ricky's birth I discovered research on evaluating the quality of life. Death equalled zero on a scale of zero to a hundred. The authors looked on a score of one hundred as perfect health and then asked people to rate various health states. What they found, to their surprise, is that many people saw certain life conditions as worse than death and gave negative numbers to represent some of these conditions. Although some people say that there is always hope for any seriously-ill person there are times when the possible advantages of hoping for cures are outweighed by the terrible condition someone must live with.

If the doctors had told us that Ricky would probably come out of their treatments blind, quadriplegic, and with no real contact with the world, we might still have decided to go ahead with the surgery because of the slim hope of improvement. The point is, we were not given the kind of information needed to make an informed decision on what was best for Ricky.

Ricky has been in pain every day since his surgery. He has been blind and deaf for most of that time although we now believe he has very limited hearing and perhaps some ability to see light. He still cannot move. He is growing in height and weight, but he has few capabilities to communicate with us about how he is feeling. He can't even laugh out loud or cry. If properly cared for he might live to a normal age.

After much discussion John and I agree that we will take care of Ricky at home. Children with his illness often get pneumonia just as Ricky has already had. Rather than bring him into a hospital where he is apt to catch other illnesses we suction his lungs at home and make him as comfortable as possible. We want him to live. Happily, my background permits us to give him care as good as he would receive in a hospital, if not better. If Ricky does die, I hope that it is in his sleep, in his own bed, after a good day. To have him tortured by more medical technology would be the worst of possible consequences.

He is in a school now for children with multiple disabilities and is getting much attention. In fact he is improving above expectations. We do not foresee a time when he will be able to take care of himself in any way but he's so darned huggable that he gives John and I a great deal of love.

We have been asked what we would do if our next child faced the same circumstances that Ricky has faced. It is a very difficult question to answer. If we had received the information the first time about what the probabilities were, we would still have gone ahead with treatment for we do believe in hope and trying. If this happened a second time, we might choose not to treat actively and help our child for as long as we could at home. It is very hard for us, knowing that Ricky is in pain every day and cannot communicate what is happening to him. The doctors now tell us that Ricky surviving the pregnancy, the operation, the coma and all his medications went against all the odds. They tried medical treatments they expected he would not survive, without telling us.

At the time it would have been easier for Ricky had he not lived and suffered as much as he has. It would have been easier for us to accept his death at such an early age knowing what was ahead of him. Now, of course, he is so much a part of our lives that we will do anything beyond further medical heroics, to keep him with us. I think we would just not want to put another child through the same thing.

Surgeons and specialists should have to live one week with the consequences of their actions. They should have to work more closely with families and nurses and other caregivers before deciding "what is best." Compassion helps people through difficult times more than the overly calm and composed temperament of the many people we dealt with, including doctors, nurses, family and friends.

Consumers should become more responsible for taking control of their medical treatment and that of their children. Doctors should learn to let go of their training long enough to look at the people they are treating and the results of their medical treatments. When patients are well enough to go home it doesn't mean that their lives rate a hundred points on the quality-of-life scale.

I am glad these attitudes are being discussed more openly today than a few years ago. I have seen incidents where there was real team work and total care given a patient. I think we can work together to make it happen in all cases; not just some cases.

CHAPTER FIVE

QUESTIONS TO ASK

Personal Medical Record
Recent Medical History
Questions Physicians Need Answered
Questions Regarding Tests
Questions About Medications
Questions To Your Physician About Your Condition
Questions Upon Entering a Hospital/Hospice
Questions Before Surgery
Medical Expense Record
Choosing a New Family Physician

The following forms and lists of questions can become your own personal medical file. Records kept by your physicians, hospital and insurance companies are owned by them, and difficult to get, therefore, they are little use to you in an emergency.

Having your own medical file will permit easy access to information by new physicians and others who need it quickly and accurately. Even if you have been a patient at a hospital before, it may take hours before your record reaches a physician and he can use it to help make a diagnosis. As it is, maintaining and storing medical records is low on the funding list of our medical system and we belong to a very mobile society where it is difficult to get records transferred from one facility to another. Therefore, maintaining your own records can save valuable time in emergency situations.

Depending on a physician's style, medical records and taking a medical history provide the information for up to 85% of a diagnosis. The other 15% comes from a physical examination and laboratory tests. An updated medical record is very important when you see a new physician but even more important during an emergency situation.

I suggest you use a black pen to fill in those sections of the forms that are unlikely to change (your name, birthdate, childhood illnesses). For information such as addresses and telephone numbers use a dark pencil so that you can easily change the information when it is necessary. Fill in only the information you want to. Information that you consider too personal can be left blank. Remember this is your medical file and you choose what goes in it. If there is information

38

you do not know (e.g. when you had the mumps), put in a question mark and your best recollection (e.g. about 1943?). Have these forms with you whenever you go to a hospital, similar medical care facility or a new physician.

Filling in forms is boring and it may also make someone feel less comfortable about her or his medical situation. Always keep in mind the uniqueness of this situation for we are dealing with someone who has a terminal illness. The forms are meant to be helpful but too much emphasis on their use can make living until death a "big production." These forms (and the list of questions) will have different applications depending upon how long someone has been ill. If they have just been diagnosed as having a terminal illness, then these forms can be very useful. If the person has been ill for a long time and under the care of the same physicians, then filling in some of the forms in great detail is not necessary. In any case, it is up to the patient and family to decide how much effort will be put into filling in these forms. If patients want the forms used but are unable to fill them out themselves, a family member or friend can help them.

There are many suggested questions in the following pages. These questions are not meant to second guess the caregivers but rather help those people who want to take an active role in their medical treatment to understand what is happening. These questions are not meant as a consumer crusade against the medical profession but rather as a means to develop a trusting, working relationship. You will not be able to ask all the questions listed because many will be answered for you or because there are time constraints. Patients can ask some of these questions of physicians while some of the other questions are best reserved for other professionals: nurses, pharmacists, therapists and others. Also the Recommended Readings at the end of this book provide several excellent reference books that will provide you with information on tests and procedures, illnesses, medications and more.

Each individual has specific needs but also individual responsibilities. The purpose of getting needed medical information is to better inform yourself before you have to make medical decisions about your own medical treatment.

Physicians and other caregivers can use the following forms and questions to encourage participation by their patients and to minimize wasted time. For example, if a patient completes a medication chart and then brings a copy of the chart and their medications to a new physician, there is little time wasted in examining and listing the drugs in the physician's file. Time can be better spent talking with the patient.

In chapter 12 there is a "Personal Information Record" which can be photocopied and included with the medical records since it provides information that might be required by hospital/hospice administrators.

PERSONAL MEDICAL RECORD

1. Name: _____

2. Sex: _____

3. Health Insurance:

    a. Type: _____

    b. Policy Number: _____

    c. Policy Owner: _____

    d. Name/Telephone Number of Agent (if applicable):

    _____

4. Date of birth: _____

5. Blood type: _____

6. Rh factor: _____

7. Language spoken: _____

8. Language preferred for reading and writing: _____

9. Name and telephone number of biological Father and/or Mother: (this information can provide necessary genetic history)

    _____

    _____

10. Height: _____

11. Weight: _____

12. Allergies (give details):

    a. To medication: _____

    _____

    b. To foods: _____

    _____

    c. To chemicals/cleaners: _____

    _____

PERSONAL MEDICAL RECORD (continued)

d. To substances (Hay Fever): _____

_____

e. Other: _____

_____

    13. For smokers:

        a. for how many years have you smoked: _____

        b. average daily amount (i.e. 20 cigarettes/day): _____

        c. if you quit smoking give date: _____

    14. Alcohol/non-prescribed drug use:

        a. type(s) of alcohol/drug: _____

        b. amount per day or week: _____

    15. Do you exercise regularily? If so, what activity and how often?

_____

    16. Average number of hours you sleep every night: _____

    17. Any religious or cultural limitations to care, (e.g. Jehovah Witnesses cannot have blood transfusions, some Jewish people require kosher meals, etc.):

_____

_____

    18. Next-of-kin:

        a. Name: _____

        b. Address: _____

        _____

        c. Phone: _____

                    Daytime   Evening

        d. Relationship: _____

    19. Family physician:

        a. Name: _____

PERSONAL MEDICAL RECORD (continued)

    b. Address: _____

    _____

    c. Telephone: _____

    d. Hospital affiliation: _____

20. Specialist physicians:

    a. Name of principal specialist; for others, use a separate page:

    _____

    b. Address: _____

    _____

    c. Telephone: _____

    d. Hospital affiliation: _____

21. Optometrist: [regarding lens prescriptions]

    a. Name: _____

    b. Address: _____

    _____

    c. Telephone: _____

22. Dentist:

    a. Name: _____

    b. Address: _____

    _____

    c. Telephone: _____

23. Pharmacist:

    a. Name: _____

    b. Address: _____

    _____

    c. Telephone: _____

PERSONAL MEDICAL RECORD (continued)

Any Physical Limitations in Mobility

1. Any physical limitation due to an injury or disease, i.e. arthritis, paraplegia, loss of limb or other limitation:

   _____

   _____

2. Difficulty with Vision? (give details)

   a. Left eye: _____

   _____

   b. Right eye: _____

   _____

3. Do you wear contact lens or glasses? _____

4. Difficulty with hearing? (give details)

   a. Left ear: _____

   _____

   b. Right ear: _____

   _____

5. Do you wear a hearing aid? _____

6. Do you wear false teeth? _____

PERSONAL MEDICAL RECORD (continued)

Childhood Diseases

Condition	Date	Complications?
chicken pox		
whooping cough		
meningitis		
mumps		
rheumatic fever		
rubella (German measles)		
rubeola (measles)		
scarlet fever		
strep throat		
others:		

PERSONAL MEDICAL RECORD (continued)

Adult Illnesses

Condition	Date	Details
Alzheimer's		
arthritis		
bronchitis		
cancer		
diabetes		
emphysema		
epilepsy		
gynecological problems		
heart condition		
migraines		
mononucleosis		
multiple sclerosis		
Parkinson's		
pneumonia		
past operations		
others:		

RECENT MEDICAL HISTORY

This file will keep your Personal Medical Record history up-to-date.

Date	Physician's Diagnosis	Treatment	Results

RECENT MEDICAL HISTORY (continued)

Lab Test Results

Date	Test	Physician	Result & Suggested Treatment

RECENT MEDICAL HISTORY (continued)

MEDICATION TIMETABLE

If you are taking various medications, a Medication Timetable will be very useful in helping you to remember what medications to take at what time during the day. Use a pencil to fill in the medication names, because your prescriptions will probably change over time. This timetable is for your personal use and not meant as a detailed list of your prescriptions (see "Prescription Drug Record" form).

Time	Medication(s)
Midnight	
1:00 (a.m.)	
2:00 (a.m.)	
3:00 (a.m.)	
4:00 (a.m.)	
5:00 (a.m.)	
6:00 (a.m.)	
7:00 (a.m.)	
8:00 (a.m.)	
9:00 (a.m.)	
10:00 (a.m.)	
11:00 (a.m.)	
Noon	
1:00 (p.m.)	
2:00 (p.m.)	
3:00 (p.m.)	
4:00 (p.m.)	
5:00 (p.m.)	
6:00 (p.m.)	
7:00 (p.m.)	
8:00 (p.m.)	
9:00 (p.m.)	
10:00 (p.m.)	
11:00 (p.m.)	

RECENT MEDICAL HISTORY (continued)

PRESCRIPTION DRUG RECORD

During treatment for a terminal illness, it is quite common to have your prescriptions changed from time to time. The following record permits you to record the kind and dose of medications you have been prescribed, how often you were to take them and the overall result of the treatment. The date and physician's name will be useful in emergency situations when your regular physician is not available to help you.

Prescription Drug Record

For example:

Date	Drug	Dosage	Taken	Physician	Result
8/1	Tylenol 3	10 mg	4/day	Kildair	pain relieved after 5 hours but returned 3 weeks later
8/23	Tylenol 3	20 mg	4/day	Kildair	pain relieved after 6 hours

Date	Drug	Dosage	Taken	Physician	Result

NOTE: Use a separate sheet of paper to write in the date and answers given to any of the following sets of questions.

QUESTIONS PHYSICIANS NEED ANSWERED

Depending on how often your various physicians see you, they will require the answers to some or all of the following. If you or a family member/friend can, write down the answers for your physician. Some physicians prefer to receive verbal answers to their questions but you can still use the written answers as a reminder of important points.

1. What specifically concerns you about your condition today?

2. What is the history of this condition? (Your Medical Record can supplement the verbal information your new physicians will require.)

3. Where in the body did the pain/symptom begin?

4. When did it start (date and time)?

5. On a scale of 1-10 with 10 equalling the worst pain you have ever had (i.e. broken arm, appendicitis) how would you measure your pain?

6. Describe any other symptoms you have had?

7. What were you doing at the time of the pain/symptom?

8. To what degree does your pain/symptom limit your normal activities?

9. How long does the pain/symptom last? (an hour, all day)

10. Is the pain/symptom constant or does it change?

11. Does the pain/symptom stay in one place or spread out to other parts of your body?

12. What makes the pain/symptom worse?

13. What makes the pain/symptom better?

14. How do the following things affect your symptoms: bowel movements, urination, coughing, sneezing, breathing, swallowing, menstruation, exercise, walking, and eating?

15. What do you intuitively feel is wrong?

16. Do you have any other information that might help me?

QUESTIONS REGARDING TESTS

Studies have shown that patients who are aware of the physical effects of a test or treatment are less afraid and recover more quickly from a difficult procedure than patients with little or no advanced information. Although caregivers may not have had a particular test themselves, they can usually provide fairly detailed information based on other patients' experiences and the medical literature on the specific test or treatment. It is important for a patient to understand why a physician has recommended a test and how the test is done. The following questions can be asked of a physician, nurse or technician to help the patient decide whether or not he will consent to the test.

1. What is the purpose of this/these tests?

2. What do you expect to learn from these tests? Will the results change my treatment in any way?

3. What will the test feel like (any pain or discomfort)?

4. What are the common risks involved in these tests?

5. Are there any after effects of these tests?

6. Can I be accompanied by my spouse/child/friend? If not, why not? (The medical world is slowly changing to permit someone to be with the patient through difficult tests. The change toward this system is similar to how fathers are now permitted into delivery rooms.)

7. Can I return home/to work after the test?

8. When will I get the results of these tests? Can I see you to go over them with you?

9. What will happen to me if I choose not to take these tests?

10. What are the chances of error or false positive/negative results? (Some tests have a high incidence of "false positives." Often tests cannot be definitive but they can help physicians know if they are on the right track.)

11. What are the costs involved, if any?

12. Other questions:

QUESTIONS ABOUT MEDICATIONS

You may ask the following questions of your pharmacist or physician. Some of the information, however, will be listed on the medication container or enclosed with the medication. Patients are responsible for thinking about these questions whenever they are asked to take new medication. Keep in mind that people react in different ways to medications while others do not follow instructions carefully enough. If you have many medications, take the time to fill in a medication timetable (see "Medication Timetable" form).

Some of the answers to the following questions can be found in any of the standard pharmaceutical textbooks listed in the Recommended Reading. If you pharmacist or physician cannot answer your questions with sufficient detail, check with one of the reference texts.

1. What are the names and purposes of these drugs?

2. What do the drugs actually do inside my body?

3. How often do I take them each day and for how many days?

4. What food, liquids, activities and other medications should I avoid when taking these drugs?

5. What are the effects of mixing these various drugs together?

6. What are the common and less common side effects of these drugs?

7. How can these side effects be controlled?

8. When should I return to give you feedback about the effectiveness of the drugs?

9. What will happen if I choose not to take these drugs?

10. What are some alternatives to taking drugs for my condition?

11. Is there a less expensive generic version of these drugs?

12. What special storage instructions should I follow? (Pharmacists usually label medication with specific instructions but you should be sure that the labels are present.)

13. Can this prescription be repeated without coming to see you again?

14. What are the costs involved? (Many prescriptions are never filled because patients do not tell their physicians that they cannot afford the medication.)

15. Do you know if my medical insurance covers any of these costs? (Ask your insurance agent or government insurance official this question.)

16. Other questions:

QUESTIONS TO YOUR PHYSICIANS ABOUT YOUR CONDITION

Once you have been physically examined and appropriate tests are done you will talk with your physician about your condition. Your family physician, as your advocate and mediator in the medical world, should help you understand the medical system. Why and how are tests done? What does the diagnosis of your condition mean to you. What treatment alternatives are there? What is the prognosis (prediction of the probable course of a disease) for your condition? What types of support (financial, physical, emotional and spiritual) are available to you?

Try to get your family physician actively involved if you have difficulty understanding or communicating with your specialists. Always make sure that you understand what your physicians are saying. It is common for them to use terms you may not understand. Physicians had to learn what these terms meant, so they can discuss them with you and help you understand them too.

In order not to waste your physician's time, it is important to ask specific questions. If you know your family physician well, you might give him a copy of the following checklist of items which you would like answered, especially if your situation has changed dramatically since your last visit.

Write down the answers to your questions so you do not have to repeat the questions at a later point. Also ask for reference material that might answer some of the questions for you. This will greatly reduce the time commitment of your physician and allow you to return later with even more specific questions and concerns. There will be times, of course, when your physician cannot give you specific answers because your disease may not be predictable. However, your physician can offer some educated guesses with recommendations of where you can go to get further information.

Diagnosis is not an exacting science because there are too many unknown variables. Physicians can usually provide educated diagnoses, however, and in cases of terminal illnesses, such as some cancers, predictability is often more accurate.

I. Diagnosis

1. What do I have?

2. What causes it?

3. How can I prevent it from happening again or getting worse?

4. Other questions:

II. Course of the Disease

1. What is the usual progress of this disease?

2. What can I expect next?

3. What other parts of my physical and mental abilities will be affected?

4. Other questions:

III. Infections

1. Can I give this illness to others and if I can, how would they get it from me (physical contact, through the air)?

2. Other questions:

IV. Other Possible Diseases

1. Could the test results and symptoms indicate a different disease than the one you mention?

2. Other questions:

V. Treatment

1. What treatment do you suggest?

2. How does the treatment work?

3. How will I be able to evaluate its success or failure?

4. How long after I begin the treatment should I see you again to report any progress?

5. How often will I need the treatment?

6. What are the side effects to this treatment?

7. What are some of the medical and non-medical alternatives of these treatments?

8. Other questions:

VI. Prognosis

Prognosis is a prediction of the probable course and outcome of a disease.

1. What is the expected outcome of this illness?

2. What will happen if I choose not to treat this illness through medication, surgery or other treatments?

3. What are the long-term effects of this illness?

4. Will I have pain as the disease develops?

5. What is an educated guess as to how long I have to live?

6. Other questions:

QUESTIONS UPON ENTERING A HOSPITAL/HOSPICE

When patients enter a hospital or hospice, it is important to remember that they are there to receive a service. They remain in control of that service by consenting to or refusing the tests and treatments offered them.

1. If English is not your first language, ask if there is anyone who can speak to you in your own language and help you understand your medical care?

2. What is the name of the admitting physician?

3. Who is the physician in charge of my case and how can I reach him or her?

4. Is the physician in charge of my case a specialist, intern, resident or medical student?

5. What special rules and regulations should I be aware of while I am in this facility?

6. What is the discharge procedure for leaving this facility?

7. Is this a teaching hospital, and if it is, will anyone be requesting that I participate in any research or educational program? (You have the right to consent or refuse to be part of any research or educational program.)

8. Does the hospital have a patient advocate office or social worker who can answer any of my questions regarding hospital procedures?

9. What costs are involved in my hospital stay, if any?

10. Other questions:

QUESTIONS BEFORE SURGERY

Surgery is a frightening proposition for most people. If patients understand the reasons for surgery, the procedures that will be followed and the results they can expect, then their fear and anxiety is greatly reduced. Again, studies have shown that patients who understand what is happening to them will recover more quickly and often feel less pain because of reduced anxiety.

1. What are the benefits and risks to this surgery?

2. What are the alternatives, their benefits and risks?

3. What is the prognosis if I choose not to have surgery?

4. What are the risks of anaesthesia in my condition?

5. What is the success rate for this surgery?

6. What are the pre-surgery procedures?

7. What happens during the actual surgery?

8. What are the post-surgery procedures?

9. Will I have much pain and discomfort after surgery?

10. What things can I expect to see so that I am not worried when I wake up, e.g. will I be on a respirator, will I have blood transfusions, and will I be in the intensive care unit?

11. What is the expected length for my recovery from surgery?

12. How soon after surgery can I go to the bathroom, eat, walk, go home, go to work, have sex, smoke and drink alcohol?

13. What are the names of the surgeons who will be operating?

14. Will there be any medical students operating? (You have the option to refuse treatment by anyone other than your surgeon.)

15. What are the costs involved, if any?

16. Other questions:

MEDICAL EXPENSE RECORD

Financial records are important to keep even if your costs are covered by insurance policies. Computer mix-ups are common and without adequate record-keeping you may have to pay an unexpected bill. Keep all receipts plus records of incidental costs such as travelling, eating out, etc.

Medical Expense Record

Date	Treatment	Dr/Hospital	Paid To	Insurance Paid or I Paid

CHOOSING A NEW FAMILY PHYSICIAN

Some people may not have a family physician to help them coordinate and understand their medical treatment. If you agree that a family physician is a patient advocate then you will also agree that who you choose to be your family physician is very important.

People have different backgrounds and experiences so you must choose a physician who best fits your needs. You must be honest with them and expect the same in return.

Check with family and friends for referrals to the kind of physician you want. Check with the local hospital for a list of physicians accepting new patients. When you meet the physician for the first time follow your intuition, for this person will represent you in the complex medical system. An inititial appointment with a new physician is really an opportunity for you to find out if you can talk comfortably with him or her and whether you feel he or she will be concerned with your needs and fears. The tone of your questions should reflect a respect for the physician while encouraging a mutual trust to develop. The main question that needs answering is whether the physician and you can work together for your health care needs.

Patients with a terminal illness or their families do not have the luxury of spending a lot of time finding a family physician. The following questions are more of a guide to help you choose someone you can work with easily. These questions should be presented in a respectful and friendly manner so that the physician understands you are trying to begin a relationship based on trust and respect. Many of the following questions can be answered by the nurse and receptionist.

Possible Questions to Ask

1. What is the physician's formal and informal training?
2. Is the physician able to care for your whole family?
3. Is the physician flexible in the length of office visits so that major problems can be discussed for more than the regular ten minutes?
4. Will the physician encourage you to learn about your illness if you want to know more?
5. Will the physician encourage participation in making medical decisions?
6. Will the physician provide reliable information on alternative therapies such as relaxation exercises, yoga, or acupuncture?
7. Does the physician agree with your opinions on such topics as modern proper pain control methods, life-support systems, and euthanasia?
8. Is the physician available for emergency house calls or phone consultations outside of office hours?
9. Who takes over the physician's case load during weekends, vacations etc.?
10. What hospital is the physician affiliated with?
11. Other questions:

CHAPTER SIX

HOSPICE CARE: THE DIGNIFIED WAY TO LIVE BEFORE YOU DIE

Definition of Palliative/Hospice Care
History of Hospice Care
Features of Hospice Care
Types of Hospice Care
Homecare Suggestions
The Hospice Care Team

DEFINITION OF PALLIATIVE/HOSPICE CARE

In today's technological society palliative/hospice care is actually a return to a more humane, patient-oriented philosophy and system of care that encourages people with a terminal illness, their families and caregivers to work together and, where possible, permits a person to die at home.

Palliative and *hospice* care are the same thing. In the United Kingdom and the United States, *hospice* is the preferred term. In Canada, *palliative* is the word used most often. For the remainder of this chapter I will use *hospice care* because it is used most broadly and is beginning to be used more often in Canada as well.

Hospice Care is as much a philosophy as it is a program or an institution. Hospice care is the active and compassionate care of people with a terminal illness, aimed at improving the quality of their remaining lives physically, emotionally and spiritually. Hospice Care is a multidisciplinary approach bringing together physicians, nurses, therapists, clerics, psychologists, and volunteers to work with patients, their family and the community.

When someone hears a caregiver say: "There is nothing more we can do." it is a frightening sentence. In fact, much can still be done to make someone's life rich and fulfilling, pain free and productive. When curing is no longer possible, caring is. About 400 B.C., Plato wrote that the mind and the body are one and should not be treated separately. In modern hospice care, the primary goal is to work with a patient and family in the three areas of physical, emotional and spiritual care.

Dr. Paul Henteleff, medical director of the St. Boniface Palliative Care Unit in Winnipeg, Manitoba, believes that dying decently is what we should be aiming at. People should feel wanted. People should not be misled by false hope. People should have the pain and symptom control they need. People should not be diverted from making the best possible end to a life — whatever that means to them.

Dr. Dorothy C. H. Ley, a founder and Past President of the Palliative Care Foundation, in Canada, agrees that hospice care is a philosophy rather than a program or service. The hospice care philosophy has been used in small and large communities alike. In fact, hospice care often develops naturally in communities where citizens have long worked together with local medical professionals, family, neighbors and fellow church members to provide total care for people who have a terminal illness. Urban centers are beginning to establish hospice programs drawing on community resources and interest to benefit the patients and their families.

Although the hospice movement is expanding rapidly, it is still almost exclusively limited to cancer patients because of the lack of sufficient beds. There are plans and new programs now to encourage participation by people with diabetes, lung disorders, AIDS, elderly people who have become very frail, children, and people who are dying but also have various physical handicaps.

At present there are approximately 1500 hospice programs in the United States and 250 in Canada. All of these programs provide some form of hospice care but may not provide in-patient facilities. To find out about programs and admitting procedures in your area, contact your physician, a local hospital or call the national hospice/palliative care organization listed in the appendix.

HISTORY OF HOSPICE CARE

Hospices were originally places of shelter provided by religious orders to pilgrims on their way to the Holy Land during the Middle Ages in Europe. Travellers found food, refuge and spiritual encouragement to prepare them for their continuing journey.

In the 19th century, Mary Aikenhead opened the first modern hospice in Dublin. She founded an order of nuns called the Irish Sisters of Charity. These sisters provided various medical and spiritual services including care for people who were dying. She began the order in her own home and coined the name, hospice. She saw death as the beginning of a journey, so her hospice was a place of refuge, just as in the Middle Ages, but for a different kind of journey.

At the turn of the century, the Sisters of Charity opened St. Joseph's Hospice in London. The spread of the modern hospice movement did not begin until Dame Cicely Saunders launched her St. Christopher's Hospice, in 1967, also in London. Dame Saunders worked in England as a nurse, then as a social worker. She met David Tasma, a patient who had a terminal illness, in a London teaching hospital. He was a Polish refugee from Warsaw. They discussed his needs for improved pain control and their ideas for a special kind of physical, emotional and spiritual care. He left her five hundred pounds to help establish such a center after his death.

Dame Saunders left social work to study medicine and trained at St. Joseph's as its first full-time medical officer. After her training she worked with the community to establish St. Christopher's Hospice. It is the oldest established terminal-care facility to combine teaching and research with patient care.

In the United States, millionaire Nathaniel Hawthorne's daughter, Rose, watched her friend, Emma Lazarus, die of cancer. (Emma Lazarus' poem is inscribed on the Statue of Liberty.) Rose Hawthorne founded the order of Dominican nuns, Servants of Relief, and opened a hospice-like home in 1899 in New York City. It wasn't until 1971, that a modern hospice program was established in New Haven, Connecticut by Dr. Sylvia Lack. Dr. Lack had studied with Dame Saunders before coming to the United States. She began with a home care program and opened a hospice center in 1978 with the support of the National Cancer Institute.

In Canada, palliative care began in the late 1960s with units in Montreal and Winnipeg. From the experiences at the Royal Victoria Hospital, Dr. Balfour Mount and his team prepared an extensive hospice care manual for professionals.

There are numerous methods of providing hospice care but the most important features are the same no matter how the service is provided.

FEATURES OF HOSPICE CARE

By definition, hospice care is anti-dogmatic, and has adapted to the needs of the patients, their families, and of a particular community. The three areas of concern in hospice care are the physical, emotional and spiritual needs of the patient and, where applicable, those of the family.

By emotional care, I include having the patient and family involved in decision making, in listening to their feelings and needs and showing them respect and compassion. Spiritual care refers more to the patient and family's concerns regarding life-after-death, their belief or disbelief in God, and encouraging the inner spiritual strength most people have regardless of their religious affiliation. Spiritual care is available through a chaplain and through the general contact between patients and families and with the other caregivers. It is up to the patient and family if they wish formal spiritual guidance and assistance.

The emotional and spiritual care offered to a patient is especially important when the patient has no family or friends nearby. The hospice caregivers are able to provide the support, understanding and compassion these person have traditionally not received in our medical system. The added comradeship possible with other patients and the opportunity to share thoughts and feelings with them, makes hospice care a vital service to these patients. For example, people with AIDS have until recently, not received the unconditional support and compassion of the community. AIDS hospices are being developed in various North American cities to meet the needs of these patients, while also educating the public about the illness and the goals of hospice care, in general.

The goal of hospice care is not to cure a terminal illness, nor to prolong life heroically. Surgical procedures are recommended only if they can help a patient's physical comfort. Few tests are carried out unless they, too, can help improve a patient's comfort. The primary concern is the comfort and caring support of patients and their family.

The most common concern of patients with a terminal illness is their fear of pain. The first priority of hospice care, therefore, is pain and symptom control. When pain is controlled, the patient can once again think clearly, love, care and feel useful. Painkillers (analgesics) are given routinely and in sufficient quantities. At the same time, medication is given to offset some of the side effects of painkillers while giving the patient maximum mental alertness.

Once pain and other symptoms of an illness are under control the patient and family have time to consider their own emotional and spiritual needs. A major concern of patients and families at this point is how a patient dies. According to Dame Saunders, proper pain and symptom control in cancer patients permits patients to be alert and communicative until a short time before death. They often slip into unconsciousness and die in the way most of us would like, in their sleep.

When we talk about emotional and spiritual care it is not an idealistic vision of a perfect world. There are very specific ways to help patients and families emotionally and spiritually. Emotional needs of people dying, their family and caregivers are described more fully in the chapter on emotional needs. Generally speaking, emotional support includes listening unconditionally to peoples' needs. This listening can be done by all the caregivers and includes having the patient and family actively involved in the decision-making process.

Often when patients are prevented from making decisions, no matter how large or small, they become very anxious, irritable, angry or unsure of themselves. They stop trusting what people close to them say. Their increased negative emotions add to their physical discomfort. Their physical discomfort adds to increased negative emotions and the vicious circle may never end. Hospice care is a way to change this circle into a positive cycle of total physical, emotional and spiritual care.

Rules are kept to a minimum. Families are encouraged to bring special meals to the person dying and eat together as a family. Cultural customs are important and respected. Family contact is crucial, so the family is encouraged to participate actively in their loved one's care.

When the patient's condition permits, frequent back rubs, walks, recreational activities, relaxation exercises, music, art and visits by friends are all encouraged. There are no specific visiting hours. Pets are sometimes allowed to visit. People are encouraged to bring their own photos, plants and other things to make them feel more at home. Patients have choices in their meals including home cooked food. They are allowed to smoke or have an alcoholic drink and are encouraged to do things they would normally enjoy doing.

Questions are answered honestly and the caregivers are respectful of a person's privacy and decisions. What we might call small things are encouraged. An example of this is that caregivers refer to their patients as Mr. or Mrs. Smith rather than "dear," or "honey." Respect is very important.

When someone dies, hospice care for the family does not end. Most hospice programs have a bereavement component which encourages continued communication with the family during their time of grief.

The caregivers' role in bereavement may begin with a letter or card signed by all the staff and sent to the family about three weeks after someone's death. There may be a follow-up call to see if the family would like to come in and visit. The family may choose to join a support group with other grieving families in order to share their feelings, anger and hopes. Respect for the family wishes remains paramount so the caregivers always leave a door open, day or night, for someone to call in and chat for a bit.

To find out about hospice programs in your community you can check with your doctor, the hospital social services department, or one of the national associations for hospices listed in the appendix. Be sure to check about costs, whether your insurance company covers some or all of the costs, and if there are competing services, to ensure that you are choosing the correct one.

TYPES OF HOSPICE CARE

The following is a list of various types of hospice care. Different communities choose different models. A program may incorporate smaller existing programs or the community may choose a specific model better suited to its needs and financial capabilities.

1) **Home care:** sometimes called hospice care without walls, this is often the key component of any hospice care program. These programs may be affiliated with a specific hospital, hospice unit or coordinated through public health agencies. Sometimes home care is strictly a community response to a need and is coordinated through a volunteer organization. In some communities the home care program is the only hospice care component available. With home care, the patient remains at home until death, rather than in a hospital or nursing home, and is treated by visiting nurses, doctors, therapists, clerics and other caregivers. Principles of pain and symptom control, emotional and spiritual care are followed.

In all hospice programs, home care is considered the most important component because people who are dying are most comfortable in their own environment. Only in situations when the family and caregivers are unable to provide quality care would patients go to the hospital or, if available, a hospice care facility.

2) Free-Standing Hospice Facility: a facility separate from any other institution providing only hospice care. Patients are often referred by a family physician or by a specialist seeing the patient in a hospital. Depending on the resources of such a facility there may be space available in emergency situations. These facilities generally do not have operating rooms, specialized life-support systems or other features of an acute care general hospital. St. Christopher's Hospice in England is the first modern example of such a free-standing hospice.

3) Free-Standing Hospital-Affiliated Hospice: a separate building housing a hospice center but affiliated to a specific hospital (often a teaching hospital).

4) Hospital-Based Unit: a separate hospice unit (also called a Palliative Care Unit) within a hospital which provides all the services of a free standing facility except that patients are within easy access of hospital personnel and facilities. Because pre-existing facilities can be restructured, such units are less expensive to begin than a free-standing facility.

5) Hospital-Based Hospice Team: rather than a separate unit within the hospital, a hospice team goes to the patients in the various wards within the hospital. The team educates the regular caregivers in pain and symptom control and encourages the emotional and spiritual care of specific patients. Hospitals with limited resources or those wishing to test the hospice program, may have only a single person introducing the program to patients and staff.

6) Extended Care Services: hospice programs in institutions such as nursing homes or chronic care hospitals.

HOMECARE SUGGESTIONS

There are numerous books on the subject of home care and what family members can do and learn to make the situation more comfortable for everyone involved. The following are a few suggestions:

1) Remember that people do not change substantially in character because of their illness. If they were easy going, caring and enjoyed a good joke before their illness they will probably be the same now. If they were unsatisfied with their lives, not easy to please and uncommunicative, they will probably not change a great deal because they are dying. Therefore treat them respectfully and give them the opportunity to direct your involvement in their care;

2) Do not try to force someone to eat. People need control over their lives and should be encouraged to make their own decisions. Patients know that food is important to living. Their diet may be prescribed but a hot plate, small cooler or refrigerator by the bed will permit them to eat many small meals when they are hungry. Also have lots of liquids readily available;

3) Daily baths, massages and general hygiene are critical for comfort but also to prevent bed sores for bedridden patients. Bed sores are very painful and almost always avoidable;

4) If conditions permit, encourage patients to decide if they wish to smoke,

drink, walk around, and have visitors. Even if these activities are tiring or un-healthy, the decision must rest with the person who is dying unless it harms someone else;

5) Although family members often want to do what is best for their loved one, they must not forget about themselves. If you feel like you are being used, say so. If you are uncomfortable with decisions that the ill person has made, be honest about your feelings and arrange for someone else to help;

6) Have a bedside bell or other device available so that patients in bed feel they have direct access to you. An ability to make contact, at their discretion, is crucial for the emotional support of patients;

7) Have music and television available should the person choose to listen or watch. People who are great sports fans, for example, may benefit from some cable television that permits them to enjoy an ongoing activity and become in-volved in something totally different from their own situation;

8) Plastic bed pans, vomit trays and the like are not as cold as metal ones;

9) Perhaps you can move the bed to the living room, den or other area where the person who is ill feels more a part of the family and every day living situa-tions. If you live in a multi-level home you might relocate the patient to a ground floor room. If the bed is near a window the person can see what is going on outside;

10) Either get a hospital-style bed or raise the one you have so that the people giving assistance do not hurt their backs;

11) For the caregivers at home, get all the assistance you need from your family, friends and professionals. Most people do not know what to do under these circumstances so they need to know how they can be helpful at this impor-tant time;

12) Buy or borrow a homecare book which gives you suggestions about how to change beds when someone is still in it, how to move someone, how to bathe a person in bed, provide good meals that discourage constipation or nausea, and other useful tips.

THE HOSPICE CARE TEAM

When people are dying of a terminal illness it is practically impossible for them to do it alone (even if they want to). Hospice care is a philosophy. As such it permits professionals and volunteers to work together to help someone who is terminally ill. Even in communities where there is no official hospice care, neigh-bors, family physicians, clerics and friends can work together as a team to help someone in need.

I will speak briefly about each potential member of this team. The nature of hospice care means constant improvements and changes so that the hospice care team in your community may include any or all of the following specialties: physicians, nurses, clerics, various types of therapists, dietitians, psychiatrist or psychologist, social workers, pharmacists, homemakers, other homecare providers and volunteers. Often, members of the hospice team, such as a psychologist or chaplain, are not full-time.

Physicians There may be one or more physicians acting as medical coordinators of the team. The special nature of hospice care has led to some physicians specializing in this field with emphasis on pain and symptom control and the physical comfort of their patients.

Nurses Nurses are the primary care-giving members of the team because they have the most contact with the patients, the family and the other caregivers. There is usually a smaller ratio between nurse and patient than in acute care general hospitals, allowing nurses to spend more time on a patient's physical comfort with back rubs, baths and such. They are also able to spend more time answering questions and listening to any comments the patient and family wish to make.

Chaplain Mother Theresa of Calcutta once said of her ministry that it was her role to take one person at a time and love that person for that time. In this way, acts of love and compassion can help make a Hindu a better Hindu, a Christian a better Christian, a Jew a better Jew, a Moslem a better Moslem, a Buddhist a better Buddhist.

Upon request, the hospice chaplain or chaplains can help patients, their family and perhaps some of the caregivers. Each patient's preference for spiritual counselling is followed. Patients may ask to speak with their own clerics, to the hospice chaplain or they may choose not to speak to anyone about their spirituality.

The chaplain often acts as an interfaith spiritual leader, spending time listening impartially to the needs and ideas of patients and their families. The chaplain also participates in preparation and performing of funeral services if the family wishes. After a patient's death, the chaplain may also continue to support the family during their time of bereavement.

The Dietitian Specially-trained dietitians can do a great deal to help provide meals that will reduce constipation and other side effects of medication. These dietitians also encourage patients and families to suggest or supply their own favorite meals such as mom's home-cooked chicken or dad's special cake. People will generally eat more if they can eat the food they are used to.

Occupational Therapists There are various therapists that can help someone with a terminal illness. Occupational therapists try to strike a balance between home management, self-care and leisure activities.

Home management includes homemaking, child care and parenting. Self-care includes personal hygiene, grooming, feeding, dressing, mobility, and adapting one's disabilities to their present needs. Leisure activities include the patient's personal interests and hobbies for self-expression and amusement.

Occupational therapists, like all other hospice caregivers, require special training so that their efforts meet the needs of their patients. The activities the patient can choose from should be offered at an appropriate time, so that grooming is done in the morning while eating assistance is offered during appropriate meal times. The activities should match a person's age, interest and needs so they are not juvenile nor disrespectful of a person's character.

Physiotherapists For every patient, the primary goal of any therapy is to keep them as independent as possible under their particular circumstances. A physiotherapist is concerned with providing physical and breathing exercises to help a patient remain independent. Exercises include limb movements, improved breathing techniques to minimize the effects of physical exertion, and recreational games. They try to avoid telling patients they cannot do something but rather let the patients decide what they can and cannot do.

Physiotherapists can also educate families and nurses in proper physical care. They use simple techniques rather than cumbersome exercise machines.

Music Therapists Music therapy can be as simple as providing patients with their favorite music to listen to. It is a scientific fact that music soothes and comforts people and can raise someone's pain threshold. Music therapy may also include active participation in playing music, listening in groups of people who share your taste in music or listening to a live performance.

Art Therapists Art therapy allows people who enjoy art to participate actively in self-expression. Many artistic forms are possible and this recreational exercise is not meant to "keep people busy and out of the way" but, rather as an enjoyable and expressive activity. Art is a way to communicate for people who have trouble verbalizing their needs.

Psychiatrists and/or Psychologists Psychiatrists and psychologists are very adaptable to the needs of patients, family and other caregivers. They usually let the patient take the lead, much as the clerics do. If the patient, family or other caregivers do not wish to see the psychiatrist or psychologist then their wishes are respected.

Dr. Stephen Fleming, an Assistant Professor of Psychology at York University in Toronto, has also served as team psychologist at a palliative care unit. He believes that psychologists and psychiatrists can be called upon to help a patient or family resolve specific problems. These problems may include interpersonal relationships, past family disputes or a patient's feelings regarding his situation, his sense of self-worth or his concerns for his family's future.

Dr. Fleming further affirms that these specialists recognize people with a terminal illness still struggle with the problems of living and need their concerns, fears and hopes addressed in a respectful and practical way. People have a future before they die and their specific concerns and needs should be addressed respecting that future.

Psychologists and psychiatrists can also help ease a patient's personal anxiety or depression which may, in turn, improve pain and symptom control. They are also called upon to help the caregivers deal with the stresses of offering care to people with a terminal illness either through individual meetings or group sessions.

Social Workers Social workers are involved in various aspects of hospice care: client advocacy, long-term therapy, crisis intervention, or short-term casework.

Client advocacy (representing the patient to other caregivers) is a key role because social workers are able to help people understand and use community resources, find sources of financial aid, and coordinate homecare services. As a patient advocate, they can also help resolve differences with other caregivers over the patient's treatment.

Long-term therapy can include discussion with the patient and family to help them with any emotional or communication difficulties they may have. The social worker may also coordinate or participate in bereavement programs for the family after a person has died.

Crisis intervention by a social worker may include helping to resolve problems that are compounded by a person's illness. An example might be helping a patient in a hospice settle a dispute with a landlord over back rent. A social worker may often offer help in cases where the patient has no family nearby or in cases where the family is unaware of ways to resolve various problems.

Short-term therapy may be one to five interviews, with the patient and/or family talking about their questions and concerns that have not been discussed with other members of the hospice care team.

Pharmacists Pharmacists can play pivotal roles in recommending medications and educating physicians, nurses, other caregivers and the patients, with their families, about appropriate use of medications. Pharmacists can also describe side effects, effects of combining medications, the effects of food and liquids on medication. They are an excellent resource.

Homemakers Depending on the jurisdiction you live in, homemakers may come from either a commercial or government agency. Homemakers can provide day-to-day services such as preparing meals, cleaning your home, doing grocery shopping and running errands. They may be in your home more than any other caregiver so it is important that the patient and family enjoy that person's company. However, it is important to remember that homemakers are not nurses and should not be expected to provide medical care.

Volunteers Volunteers are very important to an effective hospice care program. Their expertise and available time mean a great deal to the patients and family. Volunteers have often experienced the loss of a loved one or they may be interested in helping people through, what can be, a very special time of life.

Volunteers make such care possible, especially in smaller communities, by reducing the cost of providing hospice care. The use of volunteers permits full-time caregivers to concentrate on their specific areas of expertise.

Volunteers generally receive specialized training so that they become expert at listening impartially to people and offering help that the patient and family need and ask for. Volunteers do a lot of homecare visits to assure that the proper services are available and provided. They also act as a patient advocate so that the patient and family never feel alone.

CONCLUSION

The philosophy of hospice care encourages a relaxation of limits around a particular caregiver specialty so that it is not uncommon to see an occupational therapist listening to patients discuss the pain they used to have, a physician fluffing pillows, a patient comparing her religious beliefs with that of a nurse, or the chaplain helping a patient with his meal.

There are weekly meetings of the hospice care team to coordinate the overall activities of the team, during which, each team member can present or underscore a specific patient's needs or concerns. This open communication ideally keeps everyone on the team informed about each patient and family.

Of course, a patient's chart is also used to write in specific information about the patient's physical, emotional and spiritual needs. These charts are used by the different team members on different shifts to keep up-to-date on what the patient and family may need. These charts may also provide information on the patient's thoughts and feelings about her care, her fears and her hopes.

The most important people on any hospice care team are the patients, their family and close friends. Patients must choose how actively they wish to be involved in the day-to-day decisions that are made about their care. They must agree to all of their treatment. They may agree or refuse to see visitors. They should be free to express their needs. They should be free to choose the caregivers they wish to work with.

Families and close friends have vital roles to play. There are times when caregivers will forget to do something or are busy with someone else and unable to meet the patient's immediate needs. The patient's family members and friends can take turns being with the patient to make sure the patient receives proper care. Working together with the caregivers helps patients feel that their family, friends and caregivers are there when needed.

The important role of being with the patient has sometimes been called the patient advocate. This advocate can be any family member or friend who is with the patient. A more specific advocate role is played by a specific family member or friend who acts as spokesperson for the patient who may be unable or unwilling to communicate with the caregivers.

The advocate, working with the caregivers, makes sure that:

1) the patient is fed the prescribed food on time,

2) the patient's medication and treatment is accurate and given at the proper times,

3) any tests or examinations have been approved,

4) the physician and other caregivers communicate with her about all matters relating to the patient,

5) the patient is given a sense of control and respect.

The hospice movement is still relatively young and therefore constantly changing. From the patient/family point of view, it is important that you find out what services are available, what they cost and whether or not they meet your needs.

You now have an understanding of the philosophy of hospice care and can use that knowledge to help hospice care in your community. When people work together, the end result is an overall improvement of services for patients/families and increased professional satisfaction for the caregivers.

CHAPTER SEVEN

THE HOSPICE IN PRACTICE: THREE PERSPECTIVES

Helping a Parent Die: A Daughter's Story
A Nurse's Story of Caring for People Who Have a Terminal Illness
A Chaplain's Point of View

HELPING A PARENT DIE: A DAUGHTER'S STORY

I interviewed Estelle Altman because I knew that she had helped her father die two years ago and I wanted to hear what the experience meant to her. At the time, I did not know that she has a Ph.D. in Adult Education and is in private practice giving professional development training programs as well as grief therapy and family counselling. Her own personal experiences, as well as her professional knowledge, give us a clearer understanding of what it is like to lose a parent.

My father was 75 years old and originally had a cancerous tumor on his colon. It was surgically removed and the prognosis was good.

My parents lived five hours away and I convinced them to come live nearer their two children. It was difficult for them to uproot but they felt more comfortable being near their family. My father became ill again about a half-year after moving here and his cancer progressed steadily until his death in March, 1984. There were many good things that happened to us as a family during this time and a few experiences that caused a deep anger that I haven't yet resolved.

I was very fortunate with my own family. My husband was great in his support and my children were fantastic. My children were very attached to their grandparents and were able to share in their love. They were 23, 21 and 20 years old and were a great source of strength for all of us.

I had organized the family so that we could give my parents support while not totally losing our own perspective or energy. I was very close to my father and was able to arrange my practice so that I could visit him three times a day to help with his eating, go for a walk, and talk with him and my mother.

In some ways, knowing that my father was going to die gave us the opportunity to talk about many things that otherwise might have been left unsaid. There were some conflicts that needed to be resolved and we made sure that we did resolve them. My professional experience as a family counsellor and grief therapist almost got in the way of resolving some of our problems but in the end our family's need to become closer made resolving problems possible.

72

My father came from Russia. He was only a boy when he saw his father killed by the Bolsheviks. His self-esteem was not the highest because of the many experiences during his youth but during his last months he let down some of his defences and shared some of his thoughts and fears. We helped him feel his importance to us. We helped him to see his life-time accomplishments in a new way and told him how proud we were of him. We laughed together, cried together and talked more openly than ever before. It was a real time of family togetherness and love that gives us all strength and positive memories to this day.

There were difficult times, of course, and times when obvious logic had no role in what was happening to him. He was admitted to a world-renowned hospital and treated horribly. You feel degraded and helpless when you are ill, so the way your doctor and nurses treat you can have a very positive or negative impact on you. My father's doctor would yell at him and us for being too demanding about pain control and asking too many questions. I was so angry, that to this day I can't bring myself to talk to this doctor. As an adult educator I want to be able to help him see the negative effects his behavior can have on someone. I am still too angry to bring this point across in a way I think would help him.

We brought my father home and were fortunate that a social worker suggested we speak to another doctor who had more experience in pain control. When we met the new physician, he was so gentle and respectful of my father. He obviously cared about his patients' suffering and suggested that he could help. The way he helped undress and dress my father during his examination proved that he didn't consider my father as another disease to be cured but rather a man deserving of respect. It meant a great deal to us.

It was only afterwards we discovered that our new doctor was the head of a palliative care unit at another hospital. Palliative care means that the staff helps both the patient and family physically, mentally and spiritually. The doctor suggested palliative care as an option to my father staying at home, where he wanted to be. My father was frightened originally with the thought of going to a hospital but he realized that we were unable to give him the kind of physical care he required.

When my father was there, the staff's immediate concern was his pain and they were able to control it very well while still allowing him to be alert and active. This gave us an opportunity to spend more time talking with him and looking after his emotional needs.

Participating in the palliative care unit and its philosophy gave my father a new sense of self-worth. The unit was a complete contrast to traditional institutional care. Boundaries to total care are removed, schedules are flexible according to a patient/family's needs and the staff and medical treatments are non-intrusive.

My father was an active participant in living rather than consumed with thoughts of dying. When I listen to other people talk about how their parents died I feel pretty good about my father's death. I'll give you an example of how the palliative care staff adapts to the personal needs of a person who is dying. My father was Jewish but not very active in our faith in the religious sense. The hospital that my father was in is sponsored by the Roman Catholic Church but his spiritual needs were always met. The staff treated his spiritual needs with obvious caring and respect and answered any and all of the questions he had or that we had.

In respect of our Jewish customs they suggested we have our traditional Friday evening meal at the unit. This meal had brought our family together every week for years, no matter what, and it was important that we share it with my father there. We hadn't thought of asking about this because of our experiences with the other hospital. They let us use the nurses' lounge to prepare and eat the meal. They provided us with a white table cloth which is our custom. My father was able to sit at the table and share in our meal. It was very meaningful for all of us there. It was the last time my father was able to sit up before his death a few days later.

The people at the palliative care unit took some of the mystery of dying away and replaced it with facts that made dying less fearful for the rest of us. Thoughts of euthanasia didn't come up there because there was no need. When my father was at home and in such needless pain he asked to die. This was more a cry for help than a cry to die. I had told him that medication was nearby if he wanted to die but that he would have to do it himself. He chose not to kill himself and his cry for pain relief was answered at the palliative care unit.

I was asked what role our religion played. Spiritually, we got our support from each other and the loving care of the staff at the palliative care unit. Our religion did provide us with traditions and customs that gave us concrete things to do at the time of my father's illness and death and also something to hold onto at a time when our emotions were so strong. That Friday night dinner was one example.

When my father died, the Jewish traditions were all followed. Traditions were invaluable because they made decisions for us. Traditions gave us boundaries to work within. The traditions also provided ways that our family and friends could express their sorrow openly and in a comforting way. There was a book I read when my father was ill and it helped me to understand that it is quite normal to feel that the world is coming to an end and that my grief and anger are not unique but normal. I needed to be told that it is okay to have these feelings. This book looks at Jewish traditions and I highly recommend it: *The Jewish Way in Dying and Mourning* by Rabbi Morris Lamm.

I'll end with a few thoughts for other people going through similar situations. First, I would encourage you not to be afraid to try and resolve any problems or conflicts between family members. Get close to each other rather than separating until the end. Confront people with their behaviors and respect them as living people rather than someone who is "dying." It really is never too late to change things if you keep trying. There are some beautiful moments I remember that would not have happened if we did not try.

My brother was 53 and my father 75 when we went to the palliative care unit. On the way in, my brother and father held hands and that picture of two very independent people sharing feelings through touch will always be with me.

Remember that although you may be taking care of your parents, as they once took care of you, your grief and sense of loss are those of a child missing her or his parent. No matter how old you become, your parents will always be parents in your memory and in your heart. Their death, no matter how old they are, is the loss of a parent. Parents often forget that although their life is nearly over and it is only one life (as opposed to the thousands that die needlessly in war and massacres) their death means the loss of a parent to you. Remind them of that fact if they should forget.

To the people who are friends to someone who is dying, or friends to the family remaining, there are two things I recommend: first, break down the barriers that most hospitals put between you and the person. Put the side of the bed down, sit on the bed and hold a hand and give a hug. Touching says so much more than words can.

Secondly, as a friend to the family left behind, there is nothing you can do that is more comforting and reassuring than to listen, just listen. We need to talk out our loss and our anger. We don't need judgments or lectures or stories of how others cope differently. We need unconditional love and listening just as our parents do when they are dying.

A NURSE'S STORY OF CARING FOR PEOPLE WHO HAVE A TERMINAL ILLNESS

I was to meet nurse Frances Elliott (not her real name) at 11:00 a.m. for our interview at her office in the Palliative Care Unit of a large urban hospital. When I arrived, she was with a patient nearing death. She was torn between her patient and speaking to me about the palliative/hospice care philosophy.

Needless to say we agreed that I would return at a more convenient time. We had an excellent conversation when I returned and the following summarizes our chat in her little office in the place that one volunteer called the place "where there is more living going on than anywhere else."

Something that is often missed and is not emphasized enough in the literature, is the need for spiritual support of people with a terminal illness and of their families. Palliative care is the physical, emotional and spiritual care of the patient and family together.

Spiritual does not necessarily mean religious support. Rather it is an attitude and concern often expressed without words but through compassion, that touches the true person, the spirit of the individual. Patients decide whether they would like to see a chaplain or their own clergy. Non-believers may not wish to speak about religion but they often want to speak about dying and about their own beliefs. Nurses sometimes discuss their own attitudes with patients but spend more time listening to what it is their patient wishes to express. Our chaplain comes twice a day and often people with no religious inclination enjoy talking with her about things which may be other than theological, but still of the spirit.

Patients and families have two major concerns when they first come to the palliative care unit: will the patients have a lot of pain and will they die alone? The answer to both is no, for pain control techniques are such that patients are often without pain and completely alert until just a short time before their death. The families are in constant touch with us, personally and by phone, so that they can be with their loved one, day or night, if they want to be.

When a patient is very near death, the family may stay overnight and we provide them with a place to rest and up-to-the-minute information concerning their relative's condition. In palliative care, we may sometimes give the family as much care as the patient because they also have pain, fear, anger, frustration and grief. These feelings are real. We hope our involvement can be comforting and lead to an acceptance of the situation.

I don't want to give the impression that this is an idealistic place with no sorrow or negative things. People laugh, tell jokes, cry, sing, listen, share and learn but they also express anger, frustration, hate and sorrow. Overall, though, I agree with one of our volunteers who called the Palliative Care Unit the place "where there is more living going on than anywhere else."

Pain is often controlled by a morphine mixture taken orally but other medications are also used to allow the patient to remain alert, but comfortable and free of pain.

There are few rules to diminish the person's independence and patients are encouraged to visit or return home whenever possible. They leave with the knowledge that if and when it is necessary, they may return to us. Admittance to the unit is by referral, from the family physician or attending physician, to the physician in charge of the Unit and does not involve a long wait in the emergency or admitting department.

The concept of physical, emotional and spiritual care works exceptionally well and is very satisfying for the patients, their families and our staff. I have worked in the regular wards of a hospital and I am convinced that if they adopted our team approach (doctors, nurses, social workers, clergy, therapists all working together) then patients would recover faster and there would be greater job satisfaction for the staff.

Lack of information and misunderstanding may well be the major cause of complaints against a hospital and its staff rather than poor care and lack of interest. I think law suits against the medical profession and hospitals would go down as well, since people don't readily sue someone who is working with them in such a way that the patient understands what is being done and why. If the results of medical care are comfort and relief of anxiety for both patient and family, then the patient's and family's attitude to the hospital and its staff is more likely to be positive than negative.

People often ask if Palliative Care staff have greater stress than regular medical staff. They may also ask who would want to work in a place where everyone is dying. It is funny, but many of the relief staff that come to work here often ask to return. There is an openness in this unit between staff and patients that I believe should be on all wards. This is because everyone acknowledges that the patient is dying so there is very little tension present and no evasion of the fact of death.

The patient, family and caregivers understand what is happening, so it is much easier to work with patients to help them spend their last weeks or months living to their fullest potential without any secrets kept from them. At the same time, we learn a great deal from our patients and their families about loving, listening, spiritual ideas, history and what a sense a humor can accomplish. There is a freedom in this unit to try new things, to limit rules and to honestly concentrate on patients' needs. I believe this just isn't found in regular hospital wards because of the shortage of staff.

As for high staff stress, we are able to cope very well because we work as a team with no one member overruling others. We work closely with the doctors, the clergy and therapists to help the patient and family. When we have had a particularily stressful period we help each other and share common emotions and ideas. Twice a year, a nursing pyschologist comes to visit and we are able to discuss any feelings that may not have come out before. If we need any further help we only have to ask. Our support network is strong.

We have a bereavement program to help the family survivors of our patients. Three weeks after the death, we send a card to the family to say we are thinking of them. Three and six months after, we send a letter and one year later, we send a longer letter asking how the family is doing and letting them know we remember them and their loved one.

As well, family members can call us day or night for help or just a reassuring word. It may help the families in their grief to know we are still here for them. It is valuable to us, the staff, to know that we are making a positive difference in the lives of people we have worked with. Perhaps the family may need just that little knowledge of our concern to keep them going.

From a nurse's perspective, we find that nurses who work best in palliative care are those that are genuinely concerned about helping someone mentally, physically and spiritually. Nurses need a true picture of what palliative care is and what is expected of them when working in this area. It does not take them long to recognize the real benefits and personal rewards of working on such a ward.

An example of these rewards is what we learned from a 47-year-old woman who was a patient here. Actually, she was here longer than any of our patients (one year) and had cancer of the tonsils which spread upward to her face. Over time, half her face was tumorous yet she never lost a desire to live or help other patients. Her painful condition was controlled by increasing doses of morphine but she was alert until just a few hours before she died peacefully in her sleep.

She was never afraid to look in her mirror even though her youthful face was disfigured. She was usually upbeat and energetic partly because of her stoic and strong-minded character. This illness was not going to stop her from living. Whenever possible she helped with other patients or helped with some of the office chores. She joked with people but also listened, when listening was needed, to other patients.

Her major concern was her husband's well being. She knew she would die but her emphasis remained on her husband and making his life full and rich. Her husband had different shifts at work so he visited her days or nights depending on when he could get off work. The obvious love between them endeared them both to all the staff.

She was one of us; so much a part of our existence. She shared in any staff birthday festivities or parties for patients going home. Her death was difficult in the sense of loss but rewarding in that we were able to make her comfortable and share in her life. Her husband still calls every so often to see how we are doing. The rewards continue.

Palliative Care is not a "ward for the dying" but a unit for the living. A place where people often really "live" more in the several weeks or months that are left to them then they ever did before.

A CHAPLAIN'S POINT OF VIEW

I met The Reverend Keith Nevel over lunch at "the-best-kept-secret-in-town" restaurant. This beautiful restaurant with its towering ceiling, quiet and aristocratic atmosphere was the backdrop for our discussion on the role of the clergy in working with people who have a terminal illness and their families.

The Reverend Nevel is the Anglican Chaplain at a palliative care unit. He is also the Consultant on Aging for his Diocese. Just as important, he is a person with great humor and insight which put me (and I assume his patients and their families) immediately at ease. When I asked Mr. Nevel the important features of chaplaincy he was very clear. Be yourself above other things. If chaplains are uncomfortable with any aspect of aging or dying they cannot be very helpful to the people they visit.

The best a chaplain can do is to bring out the patient's own wealth of spiritual resources if the patient wants that to happen. Difficult situations, such as the death of someone you care for, challenges some people while making others feel vulnerable and alone. When they ask for our support we must provide it in an unconditional way.

Chaplains should be neutral religious figures except to members of their own particular church. Sometimes patients do not want to see me or any of the other chaplains and that is fair game. Humor allows me to ask them openly if they would like to speak with me; it also allows them to say yes or no, without feeling that I am putting them on the spot.

People all hope for a peaceful and unpainful death. I have found that the degree of peacefulness is often a measure of coming to terms with your own spiritual beliefs. I say this not in terms of church attendance but rather in how people use and understand their own spiritual resources. In my experience, I have found that people who have used religion for social reasons during their lifetime will benefit little from their faith at the time they are dying. This situation is reversible with enough time but requires people to seriously examine their relationship with God in the past and how they can strengthen their spirituality in the present.

Being an active member of a church does not protect us from difficult times, but rather, how we use the spirituality of our faith. People who have worked out their spirituality, whether in church, or not, can use their spiritual resources at time of great need. They may want to build upon their spiritual resources with a spiritual leader, like a chaplain, or they may do it by themselves or with others. Their attitude can often be expressed in the sentence: "Some people believe in the existence of God; others believe God."

People with no religion are often open to talking about spirituality because they haven't used the church as a social vehicle in the past. They are open to discussion and will debate their ideas and feelings and try to resolve any inconsistencies they may feel. One needn't accept a church's particular teachings to believe in God; whatever God may mean to that person.

One of the concerns of palliative care is the family. There is, however, a middle-class assumption that the family is always there to help patients with their death. Families often have major differences which are not immediately resolved when patients finds out they are dying. In fact, the family can often inhibit how we help patients. Our first priority is the individual patient but the family also requires our support and understanding.

We must remember that people often die the way they live. If they faced life's rewards and challenges with humor, insight, and concern for others, they will probably die in the same way. If they have been unsatisfied with their life; if they have major difficulties with their family, it is probable that they will die in the same way. People do not dramatically change because they know they are dying. If anything, their dominant characteristics become even more evident.

The chaplain's role is to offer to help both the patient and the family resolve differences, individually and together. Sometimes someone else may be more effective in helping the patient and family such as a favorite nurse, a pyschologist or a family friend. The principle here is to be flexible and meet the individual needs of the patient and family. I'll give you some examples from my own experience to make my points clear.

One of the major fears of people who are dying is that they are alone and forgotten. I visited one woman and before I could say hello she looked at my clerical collar and said: "Thank God I haven't been forgotten. Someone still cares." At times, my clerical wardrobe gives comfort to people who feel alone and my greatest joy is sharing time with them and listening to their hopes and fears without placing any judgments on them.

I mentioned how important humor can be. One man that I visited spoke about his religious experiences, good and bad. We talked about our faith, our view of an afterlife and his hopes for his family. He had not attended an Anglican service for quite some time but wanted to have communion before he died. I suggested that perhaps his family should share in this sacrament and he asked them to come the next day.

The man's wife had given him *The Joy of Stress* by Dr. Peter Hanson for Christmas and we were discussing the book when the family arrived. They were skeptical of my motives. They worried about an anticipated lecture on church attendance. To break the ice I mentioned Dr. Hanson's book and the man's wife asked me if I had read it. "I have, but I liked *The Joy of Sex* better." The family didn't know how to react until I began to laugh loudly and joyfully. The 19-year-old son joined in the laughter and we were able to talk openly and comfortably for the next half-hour. The communion was a joy to share with them. Like all church rituals, the communion service brings people together and makes a particular celebration real and concrete. It can be comforting and hopeful. It becomes a fond memory for the family after the person's death.

I receive a great deal more from the people I visit than they receive from me. During my own difficult times I look back on the lessons they have taught me. One deeply religious woman once told me about how her view of dying had changed over time. For months she had said that she was ready to die. After some introspection she discovered that what she had really meant was that she was ready for God to take her only on her terms. She would die when she was ready to go, and not a minute sooner. Her view changed. She became ready to go when God was ready to take her. Her change in perception was very comforting to her, for a heavy decision had been lifted from her shoulders. She died a most peaceful death.

I cannot speak too highly of the palliative care philosophy. The idea of spending more time listening unconditionally to patients is wonderful. Ideally, every member of the team works toward adapting the circumstances to the individual's needs.

One Roman Catholic woman had lived with a man outside of marriage for many years. She believed her actions to be "sinful" and could not speak to the Catholic Chaplain or other members of the palliative care team about her guilt. When the team found out about her situation they began to ask casual questions that permitted her to talk if she wanted to. A simple question about her frequent male visitor like: "How is he doing today?" permitted this woman to bring up a painful subject without fear of judgment or a lengthy lecture.

I have talked about how families can sometimes compound problems rather than help resolve them. I once spent many weeks talking with the young mother of an eight-year-old girl. The mother was dying of cancer and felt she had a major spiritual problem. After some discussions we found that her real problem was her father, who used her faith against her. He told her that if she was really faithful she would not have cancer. He used Biblical quotes to show her her unworthiness at a time when I was trying to help her see her own spiritual strength.

The history of this family included child abuse and the power of the father over this young mother was so negative that my efforts did not give her the great sense of peace and comfort she deserved. Fortunately, however, she was able to plan ahead for her daughter's future by arranging a guardian for her. This gave her some peace of mind. The situation was frustrating for all members of the palliative care team because we were unable to overcome the power the woman's father had over her mind.

Fear of the afterlife is another area that makes some people's deaths difficult. People who believe they have committed major sins may wish to confess them to a cleric in hopes of getting to heaven. What has surprised me most is that many of these confessions deal with decisions or mistakes someone has made decades ago. The fear of death reminds them more of their errors than of their successes.

One woman, about 55 years old, confessed to hating her step-father. Her guilt made her fear death and what her life-after-death would be like. After we talked for a while, I found that her step-father had abused her as a child and that her mother, knowing of the situation, had done nothing to protect her. She professed great love for her mother but after more chats she admitted her real hidden anger and hate. This type of confession and the talks we had afterward helped her see her life and feelings more honestly and she was better able to deal with her own death.

A few thoughts for people interested in chaplaincy work with people who have a terminal illness. The most important skill is to be yourself. Remember that the people you are dealing with are the same adults they were before they found out they were dying. Treat them with the respect they deserve, not paternalistically.

Perhaps a criticism of palliative care teams is permitted. In my own experience I have found that patients who are strong, independent and know what they want are treated differently from patients who are more ill and therefore more dependent. Staff of palliative care units give a great deal of themselves because of the nature of their work. They want to give everyone the gift of a peaceful and dignified death. When their efforts are turned down by someone more strong willed, the staff may begin to pay less attention to them than to patients who are more dependent and eager for staff's company. This is quite natural but a tendency that must be observed and addressed so that if patients change their mind about how much care they want, the option for more care is always there.

My last suggestion to caregivers, especially chaplains, is not to take yourself too seriously. Sometimes there is not enough humor in our work for we are dealing with dying people. People in the last stages of life have much to offer us. If humor can help us to put our lives and our circumstances into a larger perspective, even in the midst of the radical changes in our lives, then I am all for it. I think we can help families look back on this period in their lives with a touch of humor added to the memories of love, talking, sharing, anger, fear, frustration and every other emotion that is such a part of living.

CHAPTER EIGHT

PAIN AND SYMPTOM CONTROL

Did you know that one of the most common causes of vomiting in patients with widespread cancer is constipation? Did you know that vomiting is not the rule in patients with advanced stomach cancer?

Don't be surprised if you didn't know these facts and don't be surprised if some of your physicians don't know them either. Pain and symptom control is a relatively new field requiring specialized training. A family physician, or a specialist in cancer or heart diseases, while knowledgeable, may not know the latest techniques of pain and symptom control. It is the patient's responsibility to ensure that your physicians refer you to a pain management specialist when the need arises.

Dying with pain is perhaps the greatest fear of patients and families. North Americans are dying with pain and other undesirable symptoms because medical training hasn't kept up with medical knowledge.

In one British study, at St. Christopher's Hospice, only 66% of 607 in-coming patients with terminal illness in 1976-1977 had pain. All but ten patients obtained good pain relief. The study shows two things: people who have a terminal illness do not all suffer pain, and for the vast majority of those people who do have pain, it can usually be relieved with the person remaining alert and able to talk. Since this study even more effective pain control techniques have been developed which is very encouraging news.

The secret to pain control is giving the right drug, in the right amount, in the right way and at the right time. A person should never have to suffer pain or ask for pain relief medication. Proper medication prevents pain from returning. Once pain is managed, other symptoms like vomiting, bed sores, and dry mouths are controlled.

DEFINING PAIN

Pain is always subjective because it is what the patient says it is and not what others think it might be. Pain is a physical sensation that is modified in the mind by a patient's emotional experiences. Pain, by injury or organic causes, is relayed to the brain through the nervous system.

Pain is different than suffering and caregivers must distinguish between the two in order to provide total care to a patient. Pain control deals specifically with keeping a patient pain-free but alert. Symptom control deals more with the mental and physical suffering of patients either from symptoms such as nausea, vomiting, and bed sores or from the emotional and mental strain that accompanies a terminal illness, e.g. fear, anxiety, or depression.

Patients generally have more than one pain at a time. Along with any pain resulting from their illness they may also have arthritis, back pain, bed sores, various physical disabilities and other pain.

Pain can be broken down into three categories:

1. acute pain: toothache, appendicitis, broken leg, pinched nerve. These pains will end in a relatively short time.

2. chronic benign pain: arthritis and other similar disorders which last for more than six months but are not life threatening.

3. terminal illness pain: pain from an illness in its last stages (remember not all illnesses have pain associated with them). Pain is likely to increase over time but patients should not feel pain before their next medication is given (i.e. every three to four hours). If they do feel pain, the physician should increase their dosage or change to a stronger medication.

DESCRIBING PAIN AND SYMPTOMS

Pain is a very subjective sensation. One person's headache may force him to bed while another person's headache may allow her to continue to work. The following checklist will allow you to describe your pain and other symptoms as clearly as possible. If you or a family member/friend can, write down the answers for your doctor.

1. Where in the body did the pain/symptom begin?
2. When did it start (date and time)?
3. On a scale of 1-10, with 10 equalling the worst pain you have ever had (e.g. broken arm, back pain, severe toothache), how would you measure your pain?
4. Describe any other symptoms you have had?
5. What were you doing at the time of the pain/symptom?
6. To what degree does your pain/symptom limit your normal activities?
7. How long does the pain/symptom last? (an hour, all day)
8. Is the pain/symptom constant or does it change?

9. Does the pain/symptom stay in one place or spread out to other parts of your body?
10. What makes the pain/symptom worse?
11. What makes the pain/symptom better?
12. Other information?

PAIN CONTROL MEDICATION

I mentioned that pain has different degrees of intensity. Pain control experts divide the degrees into: mild, moderate, severe, very severe and overwhelming. At present, experts recommend the following types of medication for each level of pain:

mild	a non-narcotic e.g. aspirin
moderate	a weak narcotic e.g. codeine
severe	an intermediate-strength narcotic e.g. increased dose of codeine
very severe	a potent narcotic e.g. morphine
overwhelming	a potent narcotic and sedative e.g. diazepam.

It takes time and experimentation to arrive at the exact combination of medications that will keep a patient pain-free and alert. Patients and families can shorten this process by recording and communicating with the physician any positive or negative results of new medications.

The use of heroin versus morphine for pain control is still debated. Heroin is a concentrated derivative of morphine and therefore both act similarly within the body. Heroin is the more soluble and potent, therefore, you require less for an injection than you would of morphine. Morphine compounds are being investigated at present to improve morphine's solubility.

In Canada the use of heroin is now legal but few physicians prescribe it because they feel it is unnecessary since other, less controversial, medications are available which are just as effective, or they are afraid it may be abused or stolen. Dr. Ken Walker (writing under the name Dr. Gifford-Jones) has been a strong proponent of heroin. He states that given orally heroin and morphine are similar but when injected heroin is superior.

Heroin by injection, according to Dr. Walker, is more potent and fast acting than morphine and offers better pain relief to people with overwhelming pain in the last hours/days of their life. Heroin gives a sense of euphoria, stops lung cancer coughs, is more fast-acting, but its effects do not last as long as morphine. Dr. Walker believes heroin is an excellent option to morphine and should be treated as just another medication in the group of drugs that can help relieve pain. When new and more potent derivatives of morphine are more readily available they can replace the socially stigmatized heroin. Until that time, Dr. Walker believes heroin should be used to alleviate overwhelming pain in patients that cannot take oral doses.

Opponents to heroin use, such as Dr. Paul Henteleff of the Palliative Care Unit at St. Boniface Hospital in Winnipeg, argue that injectable pain medication is rarely used anymore. In his work he finds that less than two percent of patients require injections of any kind of pain medication while the other 98% of his patients receive pain medication orally or by way of a suppository or medication placed under the tongue. For those few patients requiring injections, he uses newer derivatives of morphine that are just as effective as heroin but were not available when the debate over heroin began years ago.

In British centers, such as St. Christopher's Hospice and Sir Michael Sobell House in Oxford, there is a move away from oral heroin use and "Brompton Cocktails" to a more simple aqueous solution of morphine. Brompton Cocktails are mixtures of morphine (or heroin), cocaine, alcohol (90%), syrup, and chloroform. Their research indicates that simpler solutions are just as effective as the more complex Brompton Cocktails and they have fewer side-effects.

Pain control through medication is an ever changing field with improvements constantly being made. It is very important that doctors treating patients with a terminal illness check with a pain control expert for the most recent recommendations. Improved pain control means improved degrees of alertness and ability to carry on daily activities for a longer time.

MYTHS ABOUT PAIN CONTROL MEDICATION

Pain control experts agree there are three myths about pain control that physicians and the general public believe in, myths which limit the effective use of medication to control pain. There is a belief that medications given at the levels experts advise will cause: 1) addiction to the drug, 2) an increased tolerance to the drug and 3) possible hallucinations from taking the drug.

Addiction to drugs during a terminal illness seems irrelevant if the drug is needed to relieve pain. Indeed, studies have shown that high levels of pain negate the addictive power of strong narcotics like morphine. When the medication is given on a regular basis to alleviate pain there are no "highs" or euphoria which is the basis of any addiction. Without such euphoria there can be no addiction. (If only we were as careful with valium and other mild tranquilizers in everyday use.)

What does occur in cases where pain becomes less because of other pain control techniques is that the body must adjust to a change in chemical dosage or removal. The morphine must therefore be slowly withdrawn, just as we would do with steroids and other medications that are not considered addictive.

Tolerance to a drug assumes that increasingly higher doses of the medication are needed to relieve pain to the point where the drug becomes ineffective. Studies by experts such as Dr. Robert Twycross of Sir Michael Sobell House in Oxford, have proven that patients can relieve pain by receiving morphine every four hours for over a year without having to increase the dosage. The key point again is that pain needs to be relieved. Too many patients have died in needless pain because of our fear of tolerance or over medicating a person. A person who has severe pain because of terminal illness wants pain relief more than anything else. It is available, but physicians untrained in this area are still hesitant to use new pain control methods. If a patient is in this situation he must ask his physician for a referral to a pain control specialist.

The fear of increased tolerance or drug overdoses leads to physicians prescribing medication on a medical chart with the abbreviation "PRN" — "when necessary." In other words, a patient must feel pain before he can ask the nurse for further medication, a situation which leads not only to unnecessary pain but also to increased anxiety and fear in a patient. The pain threshold is lowered requiring even a greater dose of medication the next time. The myth of tolerance came about because patients were made to suffer unnecessarily. According to the experts this practice of PRN must stop. Studies have shown that medication doses may have to increase over time, but at a slower rate of increase than many physicians expected.

Hallucinations do occur in about one percent of patients (this may improve with newer techniques). What has sometimes caused hallucinations, nightmares, confusion and even mania has been the use of cocaine in pain control mixtures. This practice is now stopping as cocaine has not proven to improve pain relief. The two side effects of long-term narcotic (opiate) pain control that are real and preventable are nausea and constipation. Severe nausea can be almost as discomforting as pain. Early attention to diet and medication can certainly help. Constipation causes more misery and additional health problems than almost any other side effect. It can lead to patients not eating, bowel obstructions, and confusion. It often leads to the emaciated look of cancer patients because they have not been eating. Again, early attention to diet, medication and exercise (if possible) will help.

MEDICATION RECORDS

In chapter five I presented two forms that I think can help a patient or family member keep track of medications, their dosages, and when they should be taken. These forms also permit the patient or family member to record the results of the medication. In this way the records can assist the physicians in modifying the medications when necessary. The forms are called "Prescription Drug Record" and "Medication Timetable."

OTHER PAIN CONTROL TECHNIQUES

There are other treatments for pain control. A few of these techniques use medications in a different way or use other forms of therapy such as:

1. radiotherapy: radiation is used to shrink tumors thereby reducing a patient's symptoms;

2. nerve blocks: for localized acute cancer pains, a local anaesthetic or neurolytic injection is given to block nerves from sending pain messages to the brain. Results may be temporary or long-lasting;

3. hypnosis: by oral suggestions a hypnotist can sometimes increase a person's pain threshold;

4. acupuncture: this ancient Chinese art uses sterile needles in very specific spots to neutralize pain messages going to the brain;

5. neurosurgery: with the proper use of medication and other techniques, the need for neurosurgery should be uncommon. If other measures have failed, however, neurosurgery should not be delayed.

SYMPTOM CONTROL TECHNIQUES

Total pain is not merely the sensation of pain. Total pain is a combination of physical and psychological feelings. The primary psychological component of total pain is fear. Fear can greatly aggravate a patient's physical pain, so fear, anxiety and other negative emotions must also be treated. Add to this list diarrhea, constipation, lack of hunger and energy, bed sores, lack of mobility and other symptoms and you will understand the need for symptom control and relief.

Some of the symptom control and stress management techniques that hospice care or homecare personnel use, other than medications, include:

1. diet: some foods encourage constipation while others encourage diarrhea. Knowing which foods cause what reaction can help caregivers to alleviate a specific symptom;

2. exercise: extended bed rest can lead to bed sores, constipation, back aches, general immobility and loss of muscle strength due to decreased use of muscles. Exercises, active or passive, can be done by the patient or with someone's help in bed or they can be done when the patient is out of bed. Walking, stretching and breathing exercises are excellent forms of exercise;

3. skin care: nurses that visit homes will often tell you that bed sores are one of their greatest concerns. Bed sores are very painful and almost always avoidable. They occur most often when elbows, ankles, shoulders, hips, buttocks, heels, and the back are in constant contact with a surface. Paralyzed or unconscious patients are most prone to bed sores. Proper skin care includes daily washing, skin cream treatments and the use of a lamb or sheep's skin mattress covering or water-circulating mattress pad. For people unable to move themselves in bed it is important to change their body position at least every two hours to avoid bed sores;

4. massage: gets the blood circulating, invigorates the skin and can be very soothing and or exhilarating depending on the type of massage. Everyone enjoys a massage so it is not a surprise that they are excellent for the physical and emotional well-being of a patient as well;

5. **occupational therapy:** recreational and physical activities within a patient's physical capabilities, encourages people to make decisions and participate in things that they have always enjoyed such as a walk in the garden or a card game with friends;

6. **art therapy:** for the satisfaction of doing creative work and expressing feelings. Whatever the person decides to do is fine and may end up being a gift to a grandchild or a cherished memento for a family member or caregiver.

7. **music therapy:** people can relax and be comforted by playing, listening, interpreting, and talking about music. Personal preferences are paramount to the success of music therapy;

8. **laughter:** technically it increases production of endorphins (natural chemical pain killers in our bodies), reduces tension, distracts attention, changes expectations, and is an internal jog of organs for exercise. In another sense, laughter is contagious and lets people express their feelings in a less threatening way. It can change the mood of a place faster than any other emotion. Find a few good records or videos of comedians like Bill Cosby and sit back and enjoy yourself;

9. **relaxation exercises:** deep breathing, visualization, hypnosis, meditation and prayer are all forms of relaxation exercises. They help to relax the body physically and mentally;

10. **listening:** perhaps no method of symptom control has a greater impact on a patient's fear, anxiety, loneliness and depression than someone who will listen unconditionally and who will answer questions in an honest way.

The purpose of all of these techniques is to give patients a sense of control over their lives. Even if patients become bedridden, decisions have to be made about exercises, diets etc. These decisions force patients into the decision-making process affecting their care and give them a sense of control. Independence is very important to people and symptom control helps keep them independent for as long as possible.

WHAT AFFECTS PAIN THRESHOLD?

Albert Adler's 1981 book *Psychoneuroimmunology* reports many studies that document the relationship between the mind, and the body's endocrine and immunity systems. He concludes that stress, predetermined ideas, and past experiences all affect the body in a physical way, both positively and negatively.

Pain threshold depends on a person's own inherent strength or weakness. Factors that lower a person's pain threshold are: anger, anxiety, boredom, depression, discomfort, fatigue, family difficulties, fear, frustration, introversion, insomnia, remembering past pain, and sadness.

Factors that raise a person's pain threshold are: pain relief, symptom control, sleep, compassion and understanding, relaxation, stress management, laughter, empathy, spiritual comfort, companionship, sense of purpose, and diversionary activities such as art, music, and walking.

WHAT PREVENTS ADEQUATE SYMPTOM CONTROL?

Patients' Errors:

1. believing the pain is untreatable,
2. not contacting physician for help,
3. telling physician and family that pain isn't strong,
4. failing to take medication,
5. taking medication at wrong times or not consistently,
6. fearing addiction or drug tolerance,
7. believing pain killers are only for extreme pain,
8. discontinuing medication because of severe side effects and not telling the physician.

Physicians/Nurses' Errors:

1. ignoring a patient's description of pain because it sounds exaggerated,
2. not seeing through patient's brave face,
3. prescribing pain killers that are too weak,
4. giving pain killers only when the patient says her pain has returned (effective pain control prevents the return of pain),
5. believing post-operative pain killers are suitable for cancer pain (generally, surgical pain is acute but short-lasting while cancer pain is chronic and can increase over time),
6. not giving adequate information about the medication, its use and when it must be taken,
7. not knowing enough about different types of medication and how to move from one to another as pain increases.

Conclusion To combat pain, we must recognize that pain is always real and unique for each person who has a terminal illness. Proper pain control requires the right drug or treatment, in the right way, and at the right time. Proper pain control includes some experimentation to discover the right combination of medication and treatments, requiring the complete cooperation of the patient, the family and the caregivers. When the pain is under control, other symptoms can be addressed, so that the patient's suffering is reduced and he can remain alert and active for as long as possible.

CHAPTER NINE

LEGAL AND MORAL RIGHTS AND RESPONSIBILITIES

Definition of Legal and Moral Rights
Patients' Rights and Responsibilities
Caregivers' Rights and Responsibilities
Families' Rights and Responsibilities
Resuscitation of Patients Who Have a Terminal Illness
The Living Will and The Durable Power of Attorney
Emergency Situations
"Negotiated Death"
Legal Definition of Death
Legal Concerns after Death
Complaints and Lawsuits
Medical and Hospital Insurance

DEFINITION OF LEGAL AND MORAL RIGHTS

There is a difference between the legal and moral rights of patients, family members and caregivers. Legal rights are constantly changing through legislation and case law. Legal rights are interpreted differently in each jurisdiction of the United States and Canada for each specific case and therefore I cannot list your specific rights. I will give you some general concepts of your rights but you will have to verify the specifics within your legal jurisdiction.

Moral rights refer to generally-accepted principles of care and respect that may or may not be specifically written in law. It is important to realize that moral rights are very subjective and not always arguable in courts. When issues are brought to court, the resulting decisions regarding what is acceptable care and respect of patients will depend on the laws of that specific jurisdiction as well as the details of each particular case.

To make sure of the legal rights within your jurisdiction check with: 1) your family physician or local hospital; or 2) the provincial/state medical licensing and regulatory bodies (in Canada, with the provincial College of Physicians and Surgeons or in the U.S., the state medical boards); or 3) relevant medical, professional and consumer groups listed at the back of this book; or 4) for more complex issues, with a lawyer specializing in your area of concern.

As the person with a terminal illness is the only person involved in all aspects of his medical care (tests, examinations, operations, etc.) he must take the responsibility for ensuring he receives the care and respect he deserves. Where the patient cannot act for himself, a family member or close friend can act as the patient's advocate.

American and Canadian laws stem mostly from the same English Common Law, except in Arizona, California, Florida, Louisiana and Quebec, and have many points in common, however, the specific state, provincial and national laws and procedures have developed differently in response to the society's perceived needs. Although I will present some of these differences, it remains up to individuals to determine if these rights and responsibilities are applicable to their own circumstances.

PATIENTS' RIGHTS AND RESPONSIBILITIES

Patients' Legal Rights

1. The right to be adequately informed about their illness so that mutually agreeable decisions can be made.
2. The right to consent or refuse any treatment as long as the consequences of this action are not harmful to others (i.e. authorities must treat some contagious diseases), and that such consent is based upon an understanding of the nature and risks of the treatment and any alternatives to it.
3. The right to consent or refuse treatment and to know that your consent or refusal will be followed even if you become incompetent.
4. The right to alter consent forms to include specific treatments you will or will not consent to and to list the name(s) of the specific caregivers providing the treatment (Sometimes physicians permit medical students to perform the treatment without a patient's knowledge.) Your physician may accept or reject your changes.
5. The right to receive adequate medical care under the circumstances. Although we all want to receive the best medical care available there is no workable definition for "best medical care" so the courts rely on minimum standards of care to make their decisions.
6. The right to choose one's physician if that physician agrees. Patients do not have to accept a specific physician, nor does a physician have to accept someone as a patient.
7. The right not to take part in research or teaching procedures.

Patients' Moral Rights Moral rights have some foundation in law but may prove difficult to argue in a court of law. Moral rights are more a reasonable expectation of the kind of care and treatment a patient should receive.

1. To be treated as a whole person rather than as a body with a disease.
2. To be fully informed about your condition, prognosis and treatment alternatives, unless you wish a family member or friend to represent you.

3. To be actively involved in the decision-making process at all times, retaining ultimate control over those decisions, unless you wish a family member or friend to make them for you.
4. To be respected so that your descriptions of symptoms and pain are treated seriously.
5. To be spared unnecessary tests, examinations, and treatments.
6. To be fully informed of all direct and indirect costs.
7. To be treated free of discrimination.
8. To have a second opinion upon request.
9. To have one's family and friends treated with consideration and respect.

Patient's Bill of Rights   There are numerous Bills of Patient's Rights written by consumer groups, health organizations and hospitals. They list some of the legal and moral rights of patients. In cases where communication or cooperation have broken down, these rights can be used as a basis of discussion.

Below is a copy of the American Hospital Association's "A Patient's Bill of Rights." It may serve as a general guideline to your legal and moral rights. If you use this bill or any other, in communicating with your caregiver, use it as a responsible request for open communication and improved cooperation. Also list what your responsibilities are so that it is clearly understood that you see the patient-caregiver relationship as a team effort.

American Hospital Association's "A Patient's Bill of Rights"

The American Hospital Association Board of Trustees' Committee on Health Care for the Disadvantaged, which has been a consistent advocate on behalf of consumers of health care services, developed the "Statement on a Patient's Bill of Rights," which was approved by the AHA House of Delegates February 6, 1973. The statement was published in several forms, one of which was the S74 leaflet in the Association's S series. The S74 leaflet is now superseded by this reprinting of the statement.

The American Hospital Association presents a Patient's Bill of Rights with the expectation that observance of these rights will contribute to more effective patient care and greater satisfaction for the patient, his physician, and the hospital organization. Further, the Association presents these rights in the expectation that they will be supported by the hospital on behalf of its patients, as an integral part of the healing process. It is recognized that a personal relationship between the physician and the patient is essential for the provision of proper medical care. The traditional physician-patient relationship takes on a new dimension when care is rendered within an organizational structure. Legal precedent has established that the institution itself also has a responsibility to the patient. It is in recognition of these factors that these rights are affirmed.

1. The patient has the right to considerate and respectful care.

2. The patient has the right to obtain from his physician complete current information concerning his diagnosis, treatment, and prognosis in terms the patient can be reasonably expected to understand. When it is not medically advisable to give such information to the patient, the information should be made available to an appropriate person in his behalf. He has the right to know, by name, the physician responsible for coordinating his care.

3. The patient has the right to receive from his physician information necessary to give informed consent prior to the start of any procedure and/or treatment. Except in emergencies, such information for informed consent should include but not necessarily be limited to the specific procedure and/or treatment, the medically significant risks involved, and the probable duration of incapacitation. Where medically significant alternatives for care or treatment exist, or when the patient requests information concerning medical alternatives, the patient has the right to such information. The patient also has the right to know the name of the person responsible for the procedures and/or treatment.

4. The patient has the right to refuse treatment to the extent permitted by law and to be informed of the medical consequences of his action.

5. The patient has the right to every consideration of his privacy concerning his own medical care program. Case discussion, consultation, examination, and treatment are confidential and should be conducted discreetly. Those not directly involved in his care must have the permission of the patient to be present.

6. The patient has the right to expect that all communications and records pertaining to his care should be treated as confidential.

7. The patient has the right to expect that within its capacity a hospital must make reasonable response to the request of a patient for services. The hospital must provide evaluation, service, and/or referral as indicated by the urgency of the case. When medically permissible, a patient may be transferred to another facility only after he has received complete information and explanation concerning the need for and alternatives to such a transfer. The institution to which the patient is to be transferred must first have accepted the patient for transfer.

8. The patient has the right to obtain information as to any relationship of his hospital to other health care and educational institutions insofar as his care is concerned. The patient has the right to obtain information as to the existence of any professional relationships among individuals, by name, who are treating him.

9. The patient has the right to be advised if the hospital proposes to engage in or perform human experimentation affecting his care or treatment. The patient has the right to refuse to participate in such research projects.

10. The patient has the right to expect reasonable continuity of care. He has the right to know in advance what appointment times and physicians are available and where. The patient has the right to expect that the hospital will provide a mechanism whereby he is informed by the physician or a delegate of the physician of the patient's continuing health care requirements following discharge.

11. The patient has the right to examine and receive an explanation of his bill regardless of source of payment.

12. The patient has the right to know what hospital rules and regulations apply to his conduct as a patient.

No catalog of rights can guarantee for the patient the kind of treatment he has a right to expect. A hospital has many functions to perform, including the prevention and treatment of disease, the education of both health professionals and patients, and the conduct of clinical research. All these activities must be conducted with an overriding concern for the patient, and, above all, the recognition of his dignity as a human being. Success in achieving this recognition assures success in the defense of rights of the patient.

Reprinted with the permission of the American Hospital Association, copyright 1972.

The Pros and Cons of a Bill of Rights One criticism of a Bill of Rights is that these bills imply that they represent a complete list of the patient's rights and that these rights are enforceable. They also imply that these rights are, in some way, new because they are specifically listed. In fact, many of these rights have existed for a long time in American and Canadian Common Law and in specific legislation.

Bills of Rights can discourage cooperation between patients and their caregivers because they frighten some caregivers who worry that such bills take away from spontaneous cooperation and communication.

Let's examine some specific rights and the difficulty that might arise. As I mentioned earlier, definitions of intangible terms like: reasonable standard of care, informed consent, and respectful care depend a great deal on who defines the term. If a court of law were to define these terms in each specific patient-caregiver relationship you would find as many different definitions as situations.

More specifically, worded rights can be difficult to enforce as well. Although it is wise to know a hospital's admission, treatment and discharge policies it would be impossible to list all the rules and policies of any institution.

The demand for confidentiality or privacy of medical information is difficult to enforce. Although the medical records are considered confidential they can be examined by other caregivers involved in the patient's care, and perhaps medical students, insurance companies and administrators. Patients' medical records are owned by the physician or hospital; not the patients. Patients may request to see their records and can expect cooperation but they cannot generally demand to see them without a court order.

Patients' Responsibilities Just as people have rights, they also have responsibilities. Without responsibilities, we cannot expect cooperation and honest communication with our caregivers.

Some responsibilities are:

1. To communicate honestly your symptoms, past medical history, and your own idea of what is wrong.
2. To take an active role in your own health. It is difficult to expect reasonable care if you leave all the decisions to the caregivers, because they cannot know what is going on inside you. Nor is it helpful, if you minimize the effects of treatments by abusing substances such as cigarettes, alcohol and drugs.
3. To follow your caregiver's instructions carefully after you have mutually agreed to a treatment or procedure.
4. To treat your caregivers with the same respect and consideration you expect from them.
5. To understand and respect the time constraints and other professional stresses that may affect the patient-caregiver relationship.
6. To request only tests and treatments that the physician agrees may improve your physical and emotional comfort.

CAREGIVERS' RIGHTS AND RESPONSIBILITIES

Rarely are caregivers' legal rights mentioned. Physicians, for example, do not have to accept a person as a patient nor do they generally have to provide patients with a copy of their medical record. The record belongs to the physician or hospital, not the patients.

Caregivers, physicians in particular, are given protection under the law for their medical judgment. If in their opinion a comatose patient requires life-support systems their opinion can overrule the family's wishes.

Caregivers are given a great responsibility by society and in return, their judgments are not considered legally negligent unless minimum standards of care were not followed. Extreme cases of negligence occur and should be prosecuted, however, a physician, nurse, therapist must sometimes make life-and-death decisions without the help of hindsight. Their legal rights help protect them from criminal and civil convictions. There are codes of ethics for most professional caregivers including physicians, nurses, therapists, chaplains, and psychologists. Let us look at one example to see the topics covered and what at least one profession views as its most important responsibilities.

The Canadian Medical Association's Code of Ethics

Principles of Ethical Behaviour for all physicians, including those who may not be engaged directly in clinical practice.

I Consider first the well-being of the patient.

II Honour your profession and its traditions.

III Recognize your limitations and the special skills of others in the prevention and treatment of disease.

IV Protect the patient's secrets.

V Teach and be taught.

VI Remember that integrity and professional ability should be your best advertisement.

VII Be responsible in setting a value on your services.

GUIDE TO THE ETHICAL BEHAVIOUR OF PHYSICIANS

A physician should be aware of the traditional standards established by his forebears and act within the general principles which have governed their conduct.

The oath of Hippocrates represented the desire of the members of that day to establish for themselves standards of conduct in living and in the practice of their art. Since then the principles established have been retained as our basic guidelines for ethical living with the profession of medicine.

The International Code of Ethics and the Declaration of Geneva (1948), developed and approved by The World Medical Association, have modernized the ancient codes. They have been endorsed by each member organization, including The Canadian Medical Association [and the American Medical Association], as a general guide having worldwide application.

The Canadian Medical Association accepts the responsibility of delineating the standard of ethical behaviour expected of Canadian physicians.

An interpretation of these principles is developed in the following pages, as a guide for individual physicians and provincial authorities.

RESPONSIBILITIES TO THE PATIENT

An Ethical Physician:

Standard of Care

1. will practice the art and science of medicine to the best of his ability;
2. will continue his education to improve his standard of medical care;

Respect for patient

3. will ensure that his conduct in the practice of his profession is above reproach, and that he will take neither physical, emotional nor financial advantage of his patient;

Patient's rights

4. will recognize his limitations and, when indicated, recommend to the patient that additional opinions and services be obtained;

5. will recognize that the patient has the right to accept or reject any physician and any medical care recommended to him. The patient, having chosen his physician, has the right to request of that physician opinions from other physicians of the patient's choice;

6. will keep in confidence information derived from his patient, or from a colleague, regarding a patient and divulge it only with the permission of the patient except when the law requires him to do so;

7. when acting on behalf of a third party [e.g. an insurance company] will assure himself that the patient understands the physician's legal responsibility to the third party before proceeding with the examination;

8. will recommend only those diagnostic procedures which he believes necessary to assist him in the care of the patient, and therapy which he believes necessary for the well-being of the patient. He will recognize his responsibility in advising the patient of his findings and recommendations;

9. will on the patient's request, assist him by supplying the information required to enable the patient to receive any benefits to which the patient may be entitled;

10. will be considerate of the anxiety of the patient's next-of-kin and co-operate with him in the patient's interest;

Choice of patient

11. will recognize that he has a responsibility to render medical service to any person regardless of colour, religion, or political belief;

12. shall, except in an emergency, have the right to refuse to accept a patient;

13. will render assistance in his power to any patient, where an urgent need for medical care exists;

14. will, when the patient is unable to give consent and an agent is unavailable to give consent, render such therapy as he believes to be in the patient's interest;

Continuity of Care

14. will ensure the availability of medical care to his patients in his absence; will, when he has accepted professional responsibility for an acutely-ill patient, continue to provide his services until they are no longer required, or until he has arranged for the services of another suitable physician; may, in any other situation, withdraw from his responsibility for the

care of any patient provided that he gives the patient adequate notice of his intention.

Personal morality

16. when his morality or religious conscience alone prevents him from recommending some form of therapy, he will so acquaint the patient.

Clinical research

17. will, before initiating any clinical research involving human beings, ensure that such clinical research is appraised scientifically and ethically and approved by a responsible committee and is sufficiently planned and supervised that the individuals are unlikely to suffer any harm. He will ascertain that the previous research and the purpose of the experiment justify this additional method of investigation. Before proceeding he will obtain the consent of those individuals or their agents, and will do so only after explaining the purpose of the clinical research and any possible health hazard which he can foresee;

The dying patient

18. will allow death to occur with dignity and comfort when death of the body appears to be inevitable;

19. may support the body when clinical death of the brain has occurred, but need not prolong life by unusual or heroic means;

Transplantation

20. may, when death of the brain has occurred, support cellular life in the body when some parts of the body might be used to prolong or improve the health of others;

21. will recognize his responsibility to a donor of organs to be transplanted and will give to the donor or his relatives full disclosure of his intent and the purpose of the procedure; in the case of a living donor, he will also explain the risks of the procedure;

22. will refrain from determining the time of death of the donor patient when he will be a participant in the performance of the transplant procedure or when his association with any proposed recipient might influence his judgement;

23. who determined the time of death of the donor may, subsequent to the transplant procedure, treat the recipient;

Fees to patients

24. in determining his fee to the patient, will consider his personal service and the patient's ability to pay and will be prepared to discuss his fee with his patient.

[The remaining sections of this code include the responsibilities of the physician to the profession and to society. They do not deal directly with our topic so I have not included them here.]

This code outlines the general philosophy and moral responsibilities that physicians believe their members should follow. A patient or family member, during a period when communication and cooperation with caregivers is difficult, can combine a professional code of ethics and a Patient's Bill of Rights to encourage an improved working relationship. When all participants in the relationship can agree on what each member's responsibilities are, then the patient can receive total and effective care.

FAMILIES' RIGHTS AND RESPONSIBILITIES

Many of the above moral rights and responsibilities apply to family members or close friends. Generally speaking, family members cannot go against a patient's expressed wishes for or against further treatment.

The greatest difficulties for family members arise when they wish to make decisions on behalf of their loved ones who are unable to speak for themselves. The physician may ask the family for their opinion concerning life-support systems and other treatment but their opinions do not have to be followed. Even if the patient has expressed his wishes to his family members, physicians are not obligated to listen or act upon these preferences if in their best medical judgment they should follow a different course of treatment.

RESUSCITATION OF PATIENTS WHO HAVE A TERMINAL ILLNESS

There are now various options available to patients and families in assisting the caregivers with difficult life and death decisions. The following joint statement by medical caregivers suggests a policy regarding the resuscitation of patients with a terminal illness.

Joint Statement on Terminal Illness: A Protocol for Health Professionals Regarding Resuscitative Intervention for the Terminally Ill

This joint statement of the Canadian Nurses Association, the Canadian Medical Association and the Canadian Hospital Association has been developed by a working party of the three associations in cooperation with the Canadian Bar Association, with the advice of representatives from the Catholic Health Association of Canada and the Law Reform Commission of Canada, and is based on the Statement on Terminal Illness of the Canadian Medical Association. It is intended as a basic, national guideline for use by all those involved in the care of the terminally ill. Individual institutions may wish to develop their own guidelines as an adjunct to the national statement.

Advances in medical technology are providing health care workers with increasingly sophisticated methods of resuscitation. Although interventions with these devices are often lifesaving, health care professionals often feel uncertain when deciding to resuscitate a patient for whom such an intervention would not appear to be beneficial, in that it would prolong the dying process rather than extend life.

It is recognized that there are conditions of ill health and inevitable death for which an instruction on the order sheet signed by the attending physician that there should be "no resuscitation" is appropriate and ethically acceptable. It is also recognized that it is the patient's right to accept or refuse treatment.

Therefore, in the process of caring for a dying patient it may become necessary to consider whether to resuscitate this patient, and the following protocol should be implemented.

1. Clinical criteria

1.1 When the patient's condition is such that a decision should be made as to whether a "no resuscitation" order should be written, that condition should be assessed according to certain clinical criteria.

1.2 Those criteria are the best reasonable estimates made by the responsible physician, and a second staff physician where appropriate, about the following:

1.2.1 the irreversibility of the patient's condition and/or the irreparability of the damage it has done;

1.2.2 the length of time that it can be expected that the patient will live with intervention or without intervention;

1.2.3 the consequences of the "no resuscitation" order, i.e. that it may lead to the death of the patient before the time the physician has estimated.

2. Procedural guidelines

When the clinical assessment justifies the writing of a "no resuscitation" order, the following procedural guidelines are recommended:

2.1 Decision

2.1.1 the attending physician should assess the patient's competency; unless incompetency is obvious, a second opinion should be sought.

Competent patients have the right to make decisions about their treatment. If the patient so wishes, the family members may also be consulted.

When the patient is incompetent, the appropriate member(s) of the patient's family should normally be closely involved in the decision making process.

2.1.2 The opinion of nursing staff caring for the patient should be sought; the opinion of other health care professionals involved may be sought, where practical.

2.1.3 If the attending physician has doubts about the clinical decision, a second opinion should be obtained from another physician. (There may be circumstances in which a lack of time or unavailability of another physician precludes obtaining a second opinion.)

2.1.4 A "no resuscitation" order shall be duly recorded on the patient's record.

2.2 Implementation

2.2.1 The outcome of discussions with the patient and the family, and with the hospital staff, should be recorded in the chart along with their views. The physician consultants should record their opinion as a consultant's note.

2.2.2 The health care personnel involved in the care of the patient should be informed of the decision taken and of the rationale for that decision.

2.2.3 The attending physician and the nursing staff should review a "no resuscitation" order at appropriate intervals.

2.2.4 A request by the patient to rescind a "no resuscitation" order should be implemented immediately.

2.2.5 If there are unexpected changes in the patient's condition, a nurse or another physician may rescind a "no resuscitation" order until the patient's condition can be reassessed by the attending physician.

3. Care of the patient

Palliative care to alleviate the mental and physical discomfort of the patient should be provided at all times.

Reprinted with the permission of the Canadian Hospital Association, Canadian Medical Association and Canadian Nurses Association, copyright April, 1984.

This joint statement has provided individual hospitals and professionals with the ground work upon which they can prepare their own procedures to be followed in deciding if a patient should be resuscitated in cases of terminal illness.

Resuscitation is the procedure used to help someone who has stopped breathing. In the past almost all patients were resuscitated even if they were near death and resuscitation would only prolong their suffering.

With this joint statement there is an official recognition that life-support breathing systems are not always appropriate. Check to see if your physicians have a similar protocol regarding non-resuscitation orders.

THE LIVING WILL AND DURABLE POWER OF ATTORNEY

There are several written ways patients can express their decisions regarding the kind of medical care they want. Many jurisdictions in the United States now recognize a Living Will as a legal document. Living Wills have no legal effect in Canada but can be used to interpret people's wishes about how they want to be treated when they are unable to speak.

A Living Will is a document which basically states whether people do, or do not, want to be kept alive when they are near death. The will may request, or refuse, life-support systems, special medication or heroic measures. For example, if someone with a terminal illness is near death and has pneumonia, the patient whose Living Will requested no extraordinary measures would be given medication for pain and symptom control but not treated for the pneumonia. The patient might then die "naturally" from the pneumonia.

Living Wills do not merely record people's preference for treatment, when they near death, but also serve to protect family members, physicians, lawyers and other interested parties from possible legal action if the patient's wishes are followed. With the increase in medical malpractice suits it is very understandable that caregivers would want such protection.

The Durable Power of Attorney is a further written expression of peoples' wishes. With a Durable Power of Attorney people designate someone to act for them at times when they are unable to act for themselves. This document gives the designated person the right to make medical decisions on the patient's behalf including decisions regarding life and death situations. The Power of Attorney is in effect only when the patient cannot speak for herself. It can be verbally revoked at any time.

The following sample of a Living Will and Power of Attorney is reprinted with the permission of Concern for Dying. The Durable Power of Attorney is a part of this Living Will but it can also be a separate document. I have replaced the standard Power-of-Attorney wording provided by Concern for Dying with their more detailed version. Further copies are available from their New York office (see appendix). For Canadian equivalents, contact the Dying With Dignity organizations listed in the appendix.

In the United States it is important to check with your local state laws, or one of the Right-to-Die organizations, to see if these laws require a specific style and format for a Living Will and Durable Power of Attorney. In Canada a Living Will is not legally enforceable but a Durable Power of Attorney has some legal grounds.

Although these documents have legal foundation in the United States, it is very important to remember that they are still not considered appropriate or acceptable to many medical caregivers. Both these forms can be ignored by physicians if, in their best medical judgment, the powers within the document are not appropriate for a particular patient's situation e.g., in an emergency situation when physicians do not have time to read the document or if physicians have not sent the written wishes of patients but require the cooperation of medical care-givers in order to have the effect these documents were designed for.

The Living Will (An Advance Health Care Directive)

General Information and Instructions on How to Complete Your Living Will

(Part A) General Information About a "Living Will "

Purpose of a Living Will

The Living Will is one type of advance medical directive that sets out in writing your specific wishes about consent to, or refusal of, medical treatment. The Living Will allows you to direct your family, physician and others about your choices based on your own values, wishes and beliefs.

A **Living Will** is not a Power of Attorney for Health Care. The Living Will cannot empower another person to make decisions on your behalf. For that purpose you require a Durable Power of Attorney for Health Care which must be properly completed, witnessed and dated. You will need a Durable Power of Attorney for Health Care if your family does not agree with your views on dying with dignity and are not prepared to support your directives.

Witnesses

Anyone who is competent and has reached the age of majority may act as a witness for the Living Will. They are signing that it is truly you that has completed this document and that they believe you to be competent.

Dating the Document

The Living Will must be dated at the time the person executes the document. That is, on the date both the signer and the witnesses affix their signatures.

What to Do With the Document After It Is Signed

Once the Living Will is properly completed:

- give a photocopy to your physician.
- give a photocopy to your family or a friend who is most likely to be consulted regarding your health care decisions.
- give a photocopy to your lawyer, if you wish to do so. Review the document once a year, or after any significant change in your health status, and make sure it still accurately reflects your current thinking, then initial and date the original document. If it does not reflect your current wishes, either modify the document (if you are only making a minor change) and initial the change. If you wish to make a major change, obtain new documents (see "How to obtain a new document " below).

How to Revoke Your Living Will

As long as you maintain the capacity to make your own health care decisions, you may revoke the Living Will at any time by:
a) executing a new document, (to avoid confusion, you should destroy earlier documents), or
b) a signed letter or an oral declaration to that effect, or
c) burning, tearing or otherwise destroying the original document.
IMPORTANT: If you do revoke, amend or otherwise change your Living Will in any significant way, be sure to advise anyone who may have a copy of this document that you have done so.

How to Obtain a New Document

Write or phone Dying With Dignity at the address or phone number provided. Your request will be handled promptly. If it is within your means, Dying With Dignity would appreciate your help to pay for this service.

The Wallet Card

1. **Complete and sign** the wallet size card (an abbreviation of the Living Will) when you complete your Living Will. 2. Make sure you complete the statement "the original, signed, dated document may be found... ". Explain where you keep the original Living Will (Example: "The original signed, dated document is kept in the centre drawer of my bedside table ". 3. Put the wallet card in your wallet or handbag etc. and carry it with you at all times.

(Part B) Instructions on How to Complete Your Living Will.

A Living Will is one type of 'advance directive' which may be used to express to others your wishes concerning your choice of health care should you be unable to express these wishes yourself. The Living Will directs your physician about the health care treatment you would accept or refuse under certain circumstances described in that document. As clearly as possible, you should express what is important to you in terms of an acceptable quality of life. (See below for more information on drafting of personal wishes.)

The following notes will guide you through each item of the Dying With Dignity LIVING WILL document. If you do not find the form of expression used in the document compatible with your wishes, please stroke it out and initial the change(s). If you wish to elaborate in any area, please do so and initial your addition(s).

Introduction

If any of the statements under the section "Introduction " are not in accord with your personal beliefs, amend the document accordingly.

Rights

You must be aware that it is your right to accept or refuse medical treatment. If you require assistance in stating and insisting on this right, take a friend for support when you visit your health care provider. In times of stress it can also be helpful to have a second person to listen to any instructions your health care person may provide. If you need an advocate, seek one out. This may be a social worker, a nurse, a chaplain or a family friend. Some health care facilities, nursing homes, community service centres and social service groups have advocates who would be able and willing to act in your behalf. It is YOUR responsibility to recognize when you need assistance and to seek it out.

Declaration

Self explanatory.

Circumstances, Directions, and Treatment Refusal

Study these sections thoroughly and initial those items which concur with your wishes. In the blank sections add your personal directives in your own words. Initial each addition. It is not sufficient to state only the health care you would wish or would find acceptable, you must also be clear and specific in stating what treatments you would not wish to have. If, for instance, you wish to 'live as long as possible under any circumstances', that should also be stated clearly. If there are conditions or circumstances under which you would not wish to have your life prolonged by medical means, you must say so. The more specific you can be, the more secure your family, friends and health care providers will feel about respecting your wishes. It is not necessary (and may not be helpful) to be overly detailed as you may then make it very difficult to respect your wishes. (See below for further "examples of some directive ").

IT CANNOT BE OVEREMPHASIZED THAT YOU MUST DISCUSS YOUR BELIEFS, OPINIONS, FEELINGS AND WISHES REGARDING YOUR HEALTH CARE CHOICES WITH YOUR HEALTH CARE PROVIDERS. THE MEDICAL CARE YOU RECEIVE IS CONTINGENT ON GOOD COMMUNICATION WITH YOUR PHYSICIAN, NURSE, HOSPITAL AND ANY PERSON WHO YOU EXPECT TO CARE FOR YOU.

Examples of Some Directives:

One example of a "specific " directive might be: "I am a diabetic and I know it is possible I may have circulatory and other problems in the future which would necessitate a choice regarding major surgery. I would not choose to undergo any major surgery such an amputation of a limb even at the risk of jeopardizing my life. The reason for this decision is that my experience with wound healing is very poor involving a long, protracted painful time; the suffering from such surgical intervention would not be compatible with my perception of quality of life. "

Another example: "If, after I reach the age of ____ years, and have already been diagnosed as suffering from one or more of the following conditions, and then have a cardiac arrest, I do not give permission for resuscitation to be attempted. Some of the conditions which I personally would find unacceptable include: full time confinement in an institution; permanent, irreversible blindness or deafness; incontinence of feces or urine. "

A **general type of personal directive** might be: "If I should be in a coma, with little expectation of returning to conscious, rational existence, which persists for 72 hours without significant change, I direct that life support systems of all kinds, including food and hydration, be withdrawn and I be allowed to die. "

An example of an overly detailed directive might be: "I would not wish to be treated for my diabetic condition if my blood sugar rises about 27mm/vol. and continues for 10 days, and if I am at risk of losing my sight and if my son indicates he would not be in favour of my returning to my home and would put me in a nursing home...." While these may be very important considerations for you, the way the statement is drafted may be too complex to be practical. What if only two of the conditions are met? What if there could be another option to either being at home or in a nursing home?

Die at Home

If it is your wish to die at home and not in an institution, and if this is an option for your family, friends and care givers, you may wish to include this section in your Living Will. Initial this section. If this is not an option for you, cross out this section and initial your amendment in the margin.

Liability

The signing of a Living Will is not meant to place an unreasonable hardship or liability on any other person. It is after all, his or her own freedom and right to self-determination that the signer wishes to ensure. Therefore, anyone who acts in a reasoned, caring manner in the best interest of the maker should not be subject to legal action for their intentions.

Transfer to Another Health Care Provider

Health care providers who find themselves unable to honour the directive expressed in this document, should feel obligated to transfer the care of the signer to a more sympathetic person. That person should be equally qualified. Such a transfer should be completed expeditiously and graciously and with the utmost respect for all concerned.

Transfer to Another Health Care Facility

The same principles apply here as in the case above.

Summary

You have now considered what you want to say in your personal Living Will. Complete the document as concisely as possible. However, if the circumstances you wish to describe require more space than that provided in the Living Will form, add another page and sign that page too.

Make sure the Living Will is properly signed, witnessed and dated. You may wish to note on your Living Will the name, address and phone number of your family practitioner. You may also wish to include your health care identification number. Please refer to the GENERAL INFORMATION guidelines on "What to do with the document after it is signed ".

DYING WITH DIGNITY hopes these instructions have been helpful in assisting you to complete your Living Will. Remember you may revoke or change this document at any time by following the guidelines outlined in the "General Information " section. DYING WITH DIGNITY would like to remind you to review your Living Will once a year (set a date you will remember, such as your birthday). You may also wish to initial and re-date the document in the column beside your original signature at this time.

— — — — —

The Living Will (An Advance Health Care Directive)

TO MY FAMILY, MY PHYSICIAN AND ALL OTHERS WHOM IT MAY CONCERN,

Introduction

1. Death is as much a reality as birth, growth, maturity and old age. It is the one certainty of life. However, I do not fear death as much as I fear the possible indignity the dying process may impose on me.

I realize it is possible that accidental sudden illness may bring death quickly and gently. I also realize that other circumstances may arise in which a lingering illness, or the gradual deterioration of mind and body would impose a condition or quality of life that I would find unacceptable in light of my personal values and beliefs.

After careful and thoughtful consideration I wish to state my wishes for my health care in the event I should become physically or mentally incapacitated.

Therefore, now, while I am able to exercise my right to choose the type and extent of health care which I want, I sign this Living Will as an advance directive for those who will be in a position to influence the health care to be given to me.

Rights

2. I know that when I am rational and able to express my wishes, I have the right to accept to reject any specific medical treatment. My fear is that should I lack the capacity to express my wishes, medical treatment which I do not want may be given to me.

Declaration

3. IF THE TIME COMES WHEN I LACK THE CAPACITY TO GIVE DIRECTIONS FOR MY HEALTH CARE, THIS STATEMENT SHALL STAND AS AN EXPRESSION OF MY WISHES AND DIRECTIONS.

Circumstances

Initial

4. I DIRECT THAT, IN ANY OF THE FOLLOWING CIRCUMSTANCES, I RECEIVE ONLY SUCH CARE AS WILL KEEP ME COMFORTABLE AND THAT MY DYING NOT BE PROLONGED.

___ a) AN ACUTE LIFE THREATENING ILLNESS OF AN IRREVERSIBLE NATURE, OR,

___ b) CHRONIC DEBILITATING SUFFERING OF A PERMANENT NATURE, OR,

___ c) _____

___ d) _____

___ e) _____

Directions

5. I specifically direct the following:

___ a) Give me all medication necessary to control pain even if such medication might shorten my remaining life.

___ b) Give me physical care to keep me warm and sufficiently hydrated to maintain continuous comfort.

Treatment Refused

6. In the circumstances set out in section 4, I specifically refuse the following:

___ a) Electrical, mechanical or other artificial stimulation of my heart.

___ b) Use of respiratory ventilation to assist breathing.

___ c) Artificial feeding "i.e. " by tube, intravenous or central line, other than for basic hydration.

___ d) Transfer to an intensive care or similar "high tech " facility.

(Add here any other specific medical treatment that would be unacceptable to you).

___ e) _____

___ f) _____

___ g) _____

Die at Home

Initial

___ 7. If it will not impose an undue hardship, I would prefer to die at home.

Liability

8. It is my wish that no legal action be taken against any person because they
a) acted in good faith, in accordance with the wishes expressed in this health care directive, or
b) acted contrary to the wishes expressed in this health care directive if the person did not know of its existence.

Transfer to Another Health Care Provider

9. If I should be under the care of a health care provider who, for any reason cannot give effect to my wishes, I ask that my care be transferred to another health care provider who will respect my wishes.

Transfer to Another Health Care Facility

10. If I should be a patient or resident in a health care facility which, for any reason, cannot give effect to my wishes, I ask that I be transferred to another health care facility.

_____
(Signature)   (Date)

_____
(Print Name)

_____
(Witness signature)

_____
(Print name and address)

_____
(Witness signature)

_____
(Print name and address)

—— —— —— —— ——

Instructions for Completing a Durable Power of Attorney for Health Care

For the purposes of clarity, "lawyer" refers to your solicitor or legal advisor.

"Attorney" refers to the person(s) you have delegated to act on your behalf in health care matters.

Add your complete name and address (print or type as this is not to be a signature, but rather an identification).

Item 1[*].   You may add any conditions or delete (by crossing out and initialling) any of the clauses which are inappropriate to you.

Item 8[**].   Add the name of your lawyer.

Item 8[***].   Add the name of the person(s) whom you are appointing under the Durable Power of Attorney for Health Care. You must have the permission and agreement of anyone you name. **Dying with Dignity** strongly advises that you ensure this person(s) is fully appreciative of your feelings and attitudes toward quality of life. This may require a number of conversations. Merely signing the document without consultation would defeat its purpose.

You must also be certain that the person(s) you name really will assume the responsibility you have delegated. Lastly, the person(s) you name should be reasonably accessible. For example, if you live in Toronto or Burnaby do not give Power of Attorney to a family member residing in Halifax or Mexico.

Item 9.   Repeat the name in Item 8***

The Durable Power of Attorney for Health Care must be signed (see X on last page) and dated in the presence of two witnesses, who must also sign.

You must provide your Attorney with a photocopy of this document. You should keep the original and notify your next of kin, or close friend, where it may be found. Do not keep this document in a bank vault or safety deposit box that may not be readily accessible.

You may wish to give a copy of your Durable Power of Attorney for Health Care to your family physician, or provide a copy for your hospital records if you are admitted to hospital. The primary concern is that those who might be involved in decision making, should you be incapacitated, know you have completed such a document and to whom you have entrusted this authority.

You should review your situation and the terms of this document on a regular basis with the persons to whom you have delegated this Power of Attorney.

If you have also signed a Living Will or Voluntary Euthanasia Declaration, keep these records together. Remember to re-read, initial and re-date your Living Will on a regular basis (once a year) and ensure your family, friends and attorney or lawyer know your thoughts and wishes regarding your quality of life.

— — — — —

THE DURABLE POWER OF ATTORNEY FOR HEALTH CARE:

of   _____

(name)

_____

(address)

directed to my family, my physician, my executor and all others whom it may concern.

1. I accept the inevitability of death. If, near the end of my life, I am no longer able to make decisions for my own future, if I am no longer able to communicate,

if I am unable to care for myself, if there is no reasonable expectation of my recovery from extreme physical or mental disability or incapacity, if circumstances exist that render me incapable of rational existence, if I am afflicted with irreversible injury, disease, illness, or condition,

*

then I want my attorneys to respect my wishes listed below.

Where the application of measures of artificial life support would primarily serve to prolong the moment of death, then let this document stand as an expression of my thoughts, intentions, wishes and directions–that I do not wish to endure any prolonged period of pain and suffering. I sign this document of my own free will and volition, while I am still of sound mind, and emotionally competent to make such decisions.

2. I believe in the philosophy of dying with dignity. If any of the situations specified in paragraph 1 should arise, I direct that I be allowed to die and not be kept alive by medications, artificial means or invasive measures of any kind.

3. Measures of extending life that are especially abhorrent to me, and which are to be withheld, withdrawn or discontinued if the circumstances stated in this Power of Attorney arise, include:
    (a) electrical or mechanical resuscitation of my heart;
    (b) nutritional feedings;
    (c) artificial mechanical respiration when my brain can no longer sustain breathing;
    (d) radiation, chemotherapy, and similar forms of treatment;
    (e) treatment for an illness or disease which I contracted, when I was already afflicted with a terminal illness; for example, if I were dying of [cancer] or a stroke, I would not wish any form of treatment if I contracted pneumonia.

4. I request that a "**Do Not Resuscitate**" (D.N.R.) notification be with me at all times–whether I am at home, living with family or friends, in a hospital or other care facility.

5. I do ask that medication be mercifully administered to alleviate any pain, suffering or distress even though this may hasten the moment of my death.

6. I want the wishes and directions expressed in this Power of Attorney and the spirit of this document carried out to the fullest extent permitted by law. Insofar as they are not legally enforceable, I nevertheless request that those responsible for me at such time will regard themselves as morally bound by these provisions, so that they will carry out these wishes to the fullest extent possible.

7. If it will not impose an undue burden on my family, I would like to die at home rather than in an institution.

8. I have discussed my views regarding life-sustaining measures with my lawyer

**
_____
(name)

_____
(address and phone numbers)

and with *** _____
(name)

_____
(address and phone numbers)

to whom copies of this Power of Attorney have been delivered.

9. If any of the situations specified in this document should occur, I appoint

_____

as my attorney to carry out my thoughts and wishes, including, without limiting the generality of the foregoing, obtaining a court order, if necessary, to discontinue or forbid artificial life support measures that would primarily serve to prolong the moment of my death.

10. If I should happen to under the care of a physician whose moral, ethical, or religious beliefs are not in sympathy with my wishes as expressed in this document, I direct my attorney to ask that physician to withdraw from my care, and to recommend another physician who agrees with my views on the prolongation of life. Similarly, my attorneys are empowered to transfer me to another hospital if such should be necessary to honour the directions in this document.

11. No participant in the making or carrying out of this Durable Power of Attorney, whether it be a health care provider, hospital administrator, spouse, a relative, friend or any other person, shall be held responsible in any way, legally, professionally or morally, for any consequences arising from the implementation of my wishes.

In TESTIMONY WHEREOF I have to this, my Durable Power of Attorney for Health Care, subscribed my name, this ___day of_____ 19___.

SIGNED AND DECLARED by the said

_____
(Print name)

_____
(Signature)

as and for his/her Durable Power of Attorney, in the presence of us, both present at the same time, who, at his/her request, in his/her presence, and in the presence of each other, have hereunto subscribed our names as witnesses.

_____

(name)

_____

(address)   (street)

_____

(city)   (prov.)   (postal code)

_____

(telephone)

_____

(Witness' Signature)

_____

(name)

_____

(address)   (street)

_____

(city)   (prov.)   (postal code)

_____

(telephone)

_____

(Witness' Signature)

DYING WITH DIGNITY File No:

U.S. UPDATE

Since the publication of *Choices* in 1986 there have been changes in Living Will and Declarations and Appointment of a Health Care Agent laws in the United States. The following information (updated on January 16, 1992) is reprinted with permission of Choice in Dying, formerly Concern for Dying/Society for the Right to Die, 250 West 57th Street, New York, NY 10107, (212) 246-6973.

Note: The specifics of living will and health care agent legislation vary greatly from state to state. In addition, many states also have court-made law that effects residents' rights. Contact Choice in Dying for information about specific state laws and appropriate documents for each state.

There are basically four categories of Living Will/Declarations laws and Appointment of a Health Care Agent (similar in concept to Canada's Durable Power of Attorney for Health Care):

1. Jurisdictions with legislation that authorizes both Living Wills/Declarations

and the appointment of a health care agent*: the District of Columbia, Arizona, Arkansas, California, Colorado, Connecticut, Delaware, Florida, Georgia, Hawaii, Idaho, Illinois, Indiana, Iowa, Kansas, Kentucky, Louisiana, Maine, Minnesota, Mississippi, Missouri, Montana, Nevada, New Hampshire, New Jersey, New Mexico, North Carolina, North Dakota, Ohio, Oregon, Rhode Island, South Carolina, South Dakota, Tennessee, Texas, Utah, Vermont, Virginia, Washington, West Virginia, Wisconsin and Wyoming.

2. States with legislation that authorizes only Living Wills/Declarations: Alabama, Alaska, Maryland and Oklahoma.

3. States with legislation that authorize only the appointment of a health care agent: Massachusetts, Michigan, New York and Pennsylvania*.

4. State with no refusal-of-treatment legislation: Nebraska.

* Pennsylvania has no statutory document for this purpose.

EMERGENCY SITUATIONS

Although these legal-looking forms seem overwhelming, they are just an attempt by society to simplify a very complex problem. These documents, expressing your wishes and appointing someone to speak for you, may help the decision-making process. Only recently have medical ethics become a course subject within some medical schools. There has been little formal guidance and assistance to caregivers facing life and death situations, therefore written directives of what a patient wishes can be very useful in helping caregivers make difficult decisions.

In emergency situations the physicians will have little time to study such documents so they are not very effective. However, when someone has a terminal illness, there is usually time to notify physicians and other caregivers of your concerns and wishes. Written confirmation of what you have told them will encourage more acceptance of your wishes and diminish the possibility of a lawsuit by a family member or relative.

"NEGOTIATED DEATH"

In a *New York Times* article on December 16, 1984 it was stated that "Negotiated Death" had become a fact of life in America although it remain largely unofficial. Negotiated death is simply the patient (when able), the family, physicians and perhaps nurses, hospital administrators, lawyers etc., discussing and recording what treatment is best suited for situations when a person is near death. The documents I have provided are a further assistance in this. Documentation promotes decision making without regard to the medical costs involved nor the personal preferences of caregivers. Once decisions are reached, they are recorded and reviewed as the patient's condition changes. At any point the patient may unilaterally cancel any of these decisions.

LEGAL CONCERNS AFTER DEATH

People generally have no right to will their body away. They can direct that it be used for transplants, education or research if an educational or transplant institution accepts the donation.

Survivors cannot be forced to consent to an autopsy unless the death falls within the power of medical examiners or coroners (e.g. if they suspect the death was not by natural causes).

COMPLAINTS AND LAWSUITS

There is rarely a need for lawsuits if patients, families and caregivers work together. In situations where problems occur, a lawsuit will do little to help someone who is terminally ill because it usually takes years for a lawsuit to reach the courts. Lawsuits may improve the treatment of future patients but they rarely benefit the people on whose behalf the lawsuit was filed.

Concern must remain with the person who is dying. If caregivers are not being cooperative and communicative, then speak to their superior or hospital administrator. The option of changing doctors is available to you. Bringing in a go-between like a doctor, social worker, nurse or other caregiver is an option. If you wish to complain constructively, try to speak to the person with whom you are having difficulty, to see if the problem is simply a communication problem. If that isn't effective: 1) put your complaint in writing and send it to the person you are having difficulty with and his immediate supervisor. Request their reply by a certain date; 2) list all the facts of your complaint including dates, peoples' names, and important conversations; 3) keep a copy of all letters and a diary of all communication including person-to-person conversations, telephone calls, etc.; 4) be assertive without being aggressive. Mutual respect goes farther in helping someone with a terminal illness than confrontation between patients, family and caregivers; 5) if you do not get satisfactory results, you may make a formal complaint to the physician's licensing and regulatory body. In Canada, you could contact the provincial College of Physicians and Surgeons. In the U.S., you could contact the state medical board (usually located in each state capital).

Conclusion The purpose of understanding legal and moral rights and responsibilities is simply to encourage cooperation between the patient, family and caregivers. In many situations mutual respect and understanding prevents the need to argue the letter of the law. Knowing the ground rules of the patient-family-physician relationship, however, permits people to understand what their roles are, how their roles can be improved and how, together, they can provide the total care required by someone who has a terminal illness.

EUTHANASIA

Euthanasia, like abortion, capital punishment, war, suicide, and medical experi-mentation, is a very contentious and emotional issue. People who hold strong feelings either for or against euthanasia will not change their opinions based on anything in this chapter. My purpose is to define euthanasia, examine the pros and cons as objectively as possible, and present some examples of legislative action in this field.

The title of this book is *Choices* and my goal is to present an objective discus-sion of euthanasia so that undecided people can examine the issues and make their own conclusions. If people who hold strong views for or against euthanasia can read this chapter and find arguments to support their beliefs, then I have succeeded in presenting the issues fairly.

DEFINITION

Euthanasia stems from the Greek words *eu* (well) and *thanatos* (death). It refers to a painless and happy death. In modern usuage it generally refers to the ending of someone else's life for compassionate reasons, when people are terminally ill or their suffering has become unbearable. Proponents of euthanasia argue that because of modern medical technology, it has become very difficult to die a natural death. The majority of North Americans die in hospitals where it is increasingly difficult to die as a direct result of a disease. Medical intervention, it is argued, prolongs peoples' deaths unnecessarily.

Euthanasia has been broken up into two divisions:

1) **Active euthanasia** involves someone, other than the person dying, giving that person (upon their request) a lethal dose of drugs, or ending his or her life

in any other direct way. Euthanasia by shooting or strangulation is considered "mercy killing" and is not seen as an appropriate form of euthanasia by many people who approve of active euthanasia.

2) **Passive euthanasia** involves someone, other than the person dying, choosing not to give that person life-sustaining treatment and as such has been referred to as euthanasia *by omission* while active euthanasia is euthanasia *by commission* of a direct action. Often, passive euthanasia is requested directly by the person dying, either verbally or through a written document such as a Living Will. The argument against this distinction is that, whether you directly or indirectly cause someone's death, your intention and the resulting death are the same. A doctor who chooses to let a patient die by refusing intravenous feedings, medications, surgery or a rescusitator, gets the same result as a doctor who gives a lethal dose of medication.

There is an ethical and legal debate about whether or not active and passive euthanasia are morally indistinguishable. We will use these definitions to understand how people argue the pros and cons of both these forms.

BACKGROUND ISSUES

Reasons Some People Want Euthanasia Euthanasia on the grounds of intractable or unbearable pain is becoming less of an issue. Pain control techniques are so advanced that less than one percent of people have to die in pain. Proper pain control also permits patients to remain lucid and active. The more pain control techniques are understood by physicians, the less the cry for euthanasia.

The early 20th century American feminist Carrie Chapman Catt wrote that "no grief, pain, misfortune or "broken heart" is an excuse for cutting off one's life while any power of service remains." She committed suicide during the terminal stages of her cancer after she decided she could no longer serve.

The argument for a quality of life is very important to those who support euthanasia. The basis of this argument is that individuals have the right to decide when their lives no longer have a quality that they want to live with. Defining "quality of life" is very difficult and it is unique to each individual. One person who is terminally ill, bedridden, and dependent on others will choose to live as fully as possible while someone else may ask to die.

Examining someone's quality of life can serve another purpose, however. If we know that some people are uncomfortable with their quality of life we can determine in what areas their lives can be improved through such services as hospice care, increased visits by family and friends, etc.

A last consideration for people who may choose euthanasia is the financial consideration. People who are dying worry a great deal about their families. They do not want to be an emotional burden, nor a financial one. The cost of dying in North America can be very high indeed. Studies have concluded that eighty percent of an American's medical costs are spent in the last year of their life.

Some people argue that euthanasia would allow someone to die before the horrendous costs of prolonging life bankrupts their families. This argument is an indictment of our society's inability to deal with this very real problem, and as such, it is one of the saddest arguments for euthanasia.

The Right to Die   There is a whole field of study called Bio-ethics that began around 1970. This field examines issues in medicine that are ethically, legally and/or morally contentious.

The right to die has legal foundation. A person in North America can legally commit suicide. This was not always true and at one time if someone did not succeed in committing suicide he could be charged with an offense. It is illegal, however, to help someone commit suicide, and that being the case, euthanasia is illegal in North America. Instances of active euthanasia have led to jail terms but the majority of recorded cases have led to probations or dismissals.

The question of the right to die becomes dangerously complicated when the person dying is unable to express her or his own wishes: a person, in an irreversible coma, a child severely handicapped at birth, a person who is senile.

A Handicapped Child at Birth   Often, when people argue the ethics and morals of euthanasia, they bring up the case of a child born with Down's Syndrome or another genetic disability. I separate this issue completely from the euthanasia debate because people with handicaps are generally not terminally ill as a result of their handicaps.

For example, Down's Syndrome or Spina Bifida are not terminal illnesses nor are many of the other disabilities that children are born with. We cannot realistically evaluate a child's life twenty years from now so the best guideline seems to to be; if a "normal" child receives special neo-natal care or corrective surgery for a congested heart, then the disabled child should receive the same consideration, as if his handicap did not exist. If the condition is such that treatment would prolong a painful existence then decisions about treatment can be made on those specific grounds, not on the issue of the child's disability. People live very productive and happy lives with handicaps and, therefore, should not be denied other treatments because of their disability.

In cases where the disabilities are great, consideration must first be given to the family. If they wish their child to be treated then their wishes should be accepted. If they wish their child not to be treated then the decisions should include the advice of an impartial committee of medical and social service personnel so that the child is given every benefit of the doubt.

An issue that must be faced is the financial, emotional and physical toll that having a disabled child may have on a family. It is an indictment of our society if disabled children are permitted to die because there are insufficient financial and emotional support systems available to assist families. The issue is not the right to die for disabled children, but the need for sufficient resources to assist the millions of North Americans who have a disability.

Committing Suicide Many people who argue in favour of euthanasia believe that if competent adults wish to end their lives because of their terminal illness they should have the right to commit suicide or seek the help of someone who would not be liable for such assistance.

Some people actually plan for this event by saving prescription medication. A January 12, 1986 story by CBS' "60 Minutes" examined the practice of many American senior citizens to save their prescription drugs. These people planned to use these drugs to commit suicide if they ever became terminally ill. This practice gave these people confidence in their ability to maintain control over their own lives and deaths. They worried about a painful death or an undignified old age. There are no studies to show how many of these people actually try to commit suicide later on. The important fact is that these people want control over their deaths.

The danger in using drugs and other methods to commit suicide is that many people fail in their suicide attempts and are worse off for the effort: hangings can cause paralysis, failed shootings can cause brain/heart injuries, too little or old medication can cause an irreversible coma, carbon monoxide poisoning can inflict brain damage and chemical poisoning can ruin internal organs without causing death.

THE PROS AND CONS OF EUTHANASIA

1) Con: Euthanasia, on grounds of overwhelming pain, is no longer necessary because of modern day pain and symptom control. The arrival of palliative/hospice care programs, which give people physical, emotional, and spiritual care when they are dying, negates the need for euthanasia.

Pro: Hospice care, even if it was universally available (it is not), is not an alternative for everyone. Some people may choose to die earlier even when their pain is controlled. They may prefer not to become dependent on others or they may want to avoid the further deterioration of their physical and mental abilities.

2) Con: Euthanasia allows some people to play God. It goes against our religious beliefs. Human life is sacred. Euthanasia is therefore murder.

Pro: The religious argument holds true for all those who strongly believe in it for themselves. Different religions have different views. For example, Pope Pius XII distinguished between *ordinary* and *extraordinary* measures in prolonging life. Ordinary means whatever patients can obtain and undergo without imposing an excessive burden on themselves or others. Therefore, under some circumstances, passive euthanasia through ommission of treatment, is theologically acceptable in the Roman Catholic Church.

The religious argument is also not acceptable to people who do not believe in a traditional theology, whether or not they personally believe in God.

3) Con: If euthanasia were allowed on some grounds then it will expand to other areas, i.e. wouldn't euthanasia lead to recommendations to kill old people who are no longer competent or useful? Would euthanasia permit genocide like in Nazi Germany? Would this lead to our society devaluing life?

Pro: The above concerns are real and important when examining any possible legislative changes. There are some important differences between Nazi Germany in the 1930s and North America in the 1980s:

a) Nazi Germany was a homogeneous society while North America is not. Any move to legalize active killing of incompetent people would be politically unacceptable as lobbying groups from across economic, cultural and religious lines would rise as one voice against such a horrendous policy.

b) The Nazi's genocide program, based on racial, economic and cultural bias, permitted the society to judge the value of someone's life. Euthanasia supporters believe in individuals deciding for themselves what is best. They encourage people to write down their wishes before a time when they may be unable to communicate (i.e. in an irreversible coma). Individuals, not society, determine the value of their own lives.

c) A person who is dying is not indifferent to life but, rather, can be respectful of life and respectful of a humane death. For those who believe in an afterlife, death does not terminate life; it allows a person to move on to another level of living.

4) Con: People who choose euthanasia may do so while depressed, in despair or in pain. Family members who have no love for the person, or who wish to inherit the estate may encourage someone to decide upon euthanasia "for the good of the family."

Pro: We do not need euthanasia laws to encourage unscrupulous behaviour by someone's family. It is unfortunately happening today outside the euthanasia debate. Proponents of euthanasia agree that:

a) the decision to end life must be the person's own and in his own hands (preferably written) and expressed over a period of time,

b) the decision should never be carried out during a time of depression or despair,

c) pain and symptom control should be double checked to make sure this is not the cause for the decision to end life,

d) a person's social role and relationships should be taken into account so that survivors understand the person's wishes.

5) Con: Euthanasia may end someone's life prematurely if the doctors were incorrect in their prognosis. A cure may always be found which can help someone with terminal illness.

Pro: Any prognosis of terminal illness should be substantiated by a second or third opinion. Mistakes may be made but the value that we put on life in North America will minimize the errors to a greater degree than the mistakes that are presently made through over-medication of patients and unnecessary surgery.

For a cure to be used by a patient it must go through years of tests, analysis, government approval and acceptance by the large medical establishment. Information from the doctor and various support associations will indicate what like-lihood there is of a cure being available in the patient's lifetime.

6) Con: Euthanasia is illegal and therefore the debate has no merit; as a result, it discourages individuals from taking matters into their own hands.

Pro: Passive euthanasia is legal under certain circumstances and may depend upon the patient's and family's expressed wishes. As well, laws do change, so that what is illegal one day becomes legal by the vote of our representatives the next day. In Canada, capital punishment was legal for a time, became illegal and is presently being debated to see whether or not society will accept its legality again. Laws only reflect what we want them to.

As of the end of 1986, 39 American States have Living Will Legislation that permits passive euthanias under very specific circumstances. In March, 1986, the American Medical Association's Judicial Council issued a major opinion stating that it is ethically permissable for physicians to withhold all life-promoting treat-ment, including artificial nutrition and hydration from patients who are in irre-versible comas or who have terminal illnesses

7) Con: Euthanasia goes against the Hippocratic Oath which clearly states that "I will neither give a deadly drug to anyone, if asked for, nor will I make a suggestion to this effect."

Pro: The Hippocratic Oath was modified in 1948 by the General Assembly of World Medical Associations and in 1949 in the International Code of Medical Ethics. It appeared that most physicians did not support euthanasia but more emphasis was put on permitting doctors to choose between relieving suffering over the prolonging and protecting of life in cases of terminal illness (as de-scribed in the Hippocratic Oath). In terminal illness, if giving effective pain con-trol may shorten a life it is considered ethical to do so. This argument relates more to passive euthanasia.

8) Con: People who have pain can still offer us much through their ideas, perspectives and personal histories. How much have we learned as a society from people with terminal illnesses? At some point people who are dying accept their fate and give us their insights into life and dying. Much valuable family history and caring go on during this time. Effective pain and symptom control can make this special time productive and will give many memories to help the survivors with their grieving.

Pro: Proponents of euthanasia often argue that society will end a sick animal's life but force humans to suffer needlessly. Their central argument is that individ-uals must decide for themselves if they wish to prolong their life.

9) Con: It is wrong for people to die by euthanasia, especially if they are senior citizens. Senior citizens have so much to offer us. We have not treated enough of them with the respect and dignity they deserve nor have we learned enough from them. Their desire to die prematurely is an indictment of us, not a reason for euthanasia.

Pro: Senior citizens have earned our respect and if they choose to die when they want to, they should be given that right. These people have made thousands of decisions and many of them have lived through wars, hunger and great losses. They, better than anyone, should know when and how they wish to die.

10) **Con:** The risks of legalizing active and passive euthanasia are too great to the overall population. The issue is extremely complex and the situations under which decisions may be made are too varied to write a practical law that will protect people under all situations.

Pro: Some people argue that individuals have the right to decide when and how they will die. If they can find someone (preferably a physician) who will help them, that person should not be prosecuted. Laws are made everyday around very complex issues. In the Netherlands, effective legislation has been drafted to ensure that individuals have the right to choose, or not to choose, euthanasia with the assistance of a physician.

11) **Con:** Some people will agree with passive euthanasia but they remain opposed to active euthanasia since the latter involves people in the direct killing of others with a terminal illness, even if these dying people have requested the help of someone to end their lives.

Pro: Once the decision to end life is made, there is no moral difference between withholding treatment and giving a lethal dose of medication.

12) **Con:** Since we have the right to refuse any treatment, legalizing euthanasia is unnecessary. People can just die by refusing life-saving treatment.

Pro: People can refuse treatment or commit suicide but refusing treatment can be very difficult when they, alone, are challenging the medical staff of a hospital. Refusing treatment is very difficult: in emergency situations, in situations involving children or incompetent adults, if the patients are unable to communicate, or once they are on life-support systems. Suicide is difficult to do successfully without expert advice and assistance.

LEGISLATIVE ACTION AND DISCUSSION

Euthanasia and the law became an international issue when Karen Ann Quinlan was in a car accident and entered into an irreversible coma. Her parents went to court asking that Karen's life support systems (respirator) be removed. After many months of legal battles the parents won the right to remove Karen from the respirator but Karen continued with intravenous feedings. She lived a total of ten years in coma.

Since this legal precedent in the 1970s, many U.S. States have passed legislation that permits people to write down what type of life-saving techniques they will permit in cases when they are no longer able to speak for themselves. These persons can write a "Living Will" (see sample in Chapter 9) which is legal in many, but not all states, and is not legally recognized in Canada. Notwithstanding the laws, interpretation of when a person is considered terminally ill, still provides physicians with great leeway in deciding what treatment a patient will receive.

Many hospitals have specific policies written regarding patients who are terminally ill. The most common is a protocol on non-resuscitation orders. These orders are written into patients' medical record to indicate that if they stop breathing they are not to be resuscitated.

Non-resuscitation orders avoid heroic measures when a patient is near death. Without such an order, the medical staff is obligated to resuscitate and try to restart the heart again even if a patient is obviously near death or could be considered brain dead.

THE DUTCH EXAMPLE

In November 1984, the Dutch Supreme Court stated that in cases of euthanasia, the primary judgment of using euthanasia should remain with the medical physicians. A secondary judgment always remains with the courts in cases where there is a reasonable doubt that euthanasia was carried out illegally or negligently.

In the Netherlands euthanasia is defined as the deliberate termination of an individual's life, at the individual's request, by a medical officer. Euthanasia is still illegal in the Netherlands (not prosecuted at present) but a government commission, reporting on August 19, 1985, looked at and recommended the decriminalization of euthanasia. It listed situations under which euthanasia and assisting in someone's suicide were considered acceptable. This report is before parliament but expected to be watered down to a compromise bill.

In a 1979 Dutch survey 20% of those polled believed in passive euthanasia only, 60% in active and passive euthanasia and 20% were opposed to both. In 1985, 70% wanted active euthanasia decriminalized.

According to a January 5, 1986 report by "60 Minutes," one-sixth of all deaths during 1984 in the Netherlands were by euthanasia. Physicians helping their patients to die according to the patients' wishes are not actively prosecuted for doing this. Death is by a lethal injection after the physician carefully, and over time, determines if the patient is sincere in his or her wish to die.

The Dutch Medical Association presumes 1) that euthanasia is practiced by physicians, 2) that it embraces all measures aimed at ending peoples' lives at their own request, 3) that it should only be done by a licensed physician, 4) that physicians must verify the sincerity of the patient's wish, 5) that the wish to die is expressed voluntarily, and 6) that the wish is enduring and well considered. These physicians also believe that an independent evaluation procedure for a second opinion should be installed. Physicians should also be permitted to put on the death certificate the specific cause of death (euthanasia) rather than just the terminal illness.

THE AMERICAN EXAMPLE

Although many forms of euthanasia remain illegal in the United States there is a practice going on called "Negotiated Death." The *New York Times* reported in December, 1984 that negotiated deaths have become a fact of American life. In negotiated death, patients (if able), their family, one or two doctors, possibly the hospital administrator and perhaps family and hospital lawyers all get together to discuss a patient's case and under what circumstances extraordinary measures will no longer be used to keep the patient alive. Their agreement may or may not be recorded in the medical record and the decision can be changed at any time when the patient's situation improves or deteriorates.

Others have suggested that this practice become official. A committee could be established in cases where patients are unable to speak for themselves. The committee would include a family member, two or more physicians, one or more nurses, a cleric and/or social worker, and someone with legal expertise. If possible a lay person who has faced a similar situation could aid the family.

In an emergency (accident, severe heart attack or stroke), the family and a smaller number of participants from the Emergency Department of a hospital would act as the committee for a patient who is terminally ill.

In any and all cases, the decision to end further medical treatment would be recorded on the medical chart and could be changed at any time when the circumstances differ. If patients become able to communicate, their decision would be final.

CONCLUSION

Euthanasia is a subject that can never receive unanimous support either for or against it. People who wish to legalize euthanasia are, on the whole, as respectful of life as those who oppose it. The philosophies on both sides of the debate are very different but there is a common ground; most people involved in this debate want to improve the lives of people who have a terminal illness. The debate is helping us to examine our own beliefs while also encouraging us to improve present services to people who have a terminal illness.

CHAPTER ELEVEN

EMOTIONAL ASPECTS OF DEATH AND DYING

The Needs and Feelings of Someone Who is Dying
Children and Dying
Family and Friends
Grieving
Caregiver Stresses
Letters Written to Family, Friends and Colleagues

Young men fear death — old men fear dying.
— Hippocrates

Three groups of people are affected when someone is dying: the person who is dying, the family and friends, and the caregivers. Emotional aspects must be considered both before someone's death and after. There are many books written on the emotional and psychological effects of death and dying. The Recommended Readings at the end of this book provides an extensive list of useful books.

From the research done in this field, it is clear that the best thing that people can do during a difficult emotional time is to share their feelings and needs with others. Speaking with family and friends, a cleric and/or professional counsellors will help people to air their feelings, look at their choices and understand more clearly what is happening to them.

Let's look at some general stress management recommendations that may be used and then look at some specific situations.

THE NEEDS AND FEELINGS OF SOMEONE WHO IS DYING

It will come as no surprise that there are numerous studies describing what someone who is dying feels and needs. What has not been made clear, however, is that people do not fundamentally change their character once they know they have a terminal illness. If they were happy and able to communicate openly before finding out that they have a terminal illness, they will probably continue to do so. If they are quiet and reflective by nature, they will probably stay that way.

126

In fact, finding out about terminal illness changes someone less than it does the people around them. Family and friends will treat someone who is dying differently unless they are made aware that the person has not changed dramatically. Because someone is terminally ill does not mean that she is unable to work, play, talk, sing, tell jokes, laugh, swear, have sex, eat her favorite meals and be the person she has always been. There is no reason to give up sex, socializing, and work unless physical conditions makes it impossible. Yet many people do give up many of these things because of social expectations that they should be resting in bed, conserving their energy or fighting depression. A person's abilities will decrease as the illness progresses but there are often years or months of productive life before overall lifestyle is drastically reduced. Open communication will let others know what the person can do, wants to do and still enjoys doing.

For people who are dying it is often very difficult to tell their family and friends what they need and want. It may be difficult for your family and friends to discuss such matters as sex or going on a vacation together. Patience is required to encourage discussion. Telling a friend that you need a hug or asking a family member to go for a long walk to talk about "the good old days" are just two examples of asking to have your needs fulfilled.

Sex will depend on patients' previous experiences of having sex during stressful times, the presence of pain and medication, the perception of their ability to live a full and meaningful life and how other people treat them. If their physical or mental condition precludes intercourse, a fulfilling and caring intimacy can still happen under the comfort of touching and love. A snuggle on the couch, watching a sunset or listening to classical music together can be very intimate and loving.

Patients can choose to make decisions and take control of their lives by finding out more about their illness, how it progresses, what pain and symptom control techniques are applicable, alternatives to traditional medicine and other relevant information. They shouldn't be afraid to ask for help from a family member or friend.

In order to understand what a patient is going through, doctors, psychologists and others have tried to label your feelings. One of the first notable mentions of "stages of dying" was in Dr. Elisabeth Kubler-Ross' 1969 book, *On Death and Dying*. She believed that when people hear they are going to die they go through the following stages: denial, anger, bargaining, depression and acceptance. Research shows that some people may stay in only one stage, e.g. denial of their dying, until their death. Others may move between anger, denial, depression back to anger and then acceptance.

Dr. Avery Weisman, in his 1972 book *On Dying and Denying,* reported that people follow no predictable sequence of emotions. He believes that people fluctuate from one emotion to another depending on their individual circumstances. He has studied extensively in this field and concludes that people progress through three psychosocial stages during which a person's overall emotions do change: 1) primary recognition and denial of the illness; 2) a relatively lengthy intermediate period when the disease will progress, with possible arrests and relapses, resulting in changes of feelings from joy to sorrow, anger to frustration, hope to despair; and 3) the final decline when the person gives over control of his or her life to others and denies the concept of extinction while worrying about the image of death. The individual circumstances and characteristics of the person influence the degree to which he denies his illness and then his death. Many people progress from denying their illness and death to acceptance of the inevitable.

Labelling feelings can help all of us face the truth about dying, and denial can also be very beneficial. Take the example of a woman riddled with cancer who refused to die until her daughter reached 18 years of age. She went against all medical odds and accomplished her goal. Knowing the strength of denial or anger or acceptance can help us talk about what we are doing and why we are doing it.

The danger in labelling stages is that some people may assume that patients' emotions all stem from their knowledge of their impending death. They may be in a hospital and be very angry that a family member hasn't visited as promised or that the doctor failed to see them today. They may be depressed because a friend at work has had a heart attack. If their television is broken and the repair person doesn't come on time their anger is not because of their illness. These emotions are related to the things that they normally would react to.

There are basically three things people who are dying need, according to experts like Robert E. Kavanaugh:
1. to be accepted and respected as the people they are rather than the dying person other people see;
2. permission to die from all the important people in their lives. People who are dying do not want their loved ones to be angry or deny that they are dying because it will make their illness and saying goodbye too difficult. Loved ones need to accept the truth that the person is dying. Pretending otherwise puts up barriers to communication. People end up isolating each other because they cannot talk about their loneliness, hopes, fear and feelings of love;
3. a need to voluntarily let go of every person and possession that they hold dear. People need to say goodbye to their families, their friends, and their material possessions (photos, hobbies, books).

What can make an acceptance of death difficult is a fear of an afterlife. What will happen to them when they die? Is there a heaven? Is there a hell? Will my spirit leave my body? One doesn't need a specific religion to look forward to or fear an afterlife. If people are concerned about an afterlife, they need to talk to someone who accepts their view of God and the world that may exist after death. A chaplain, a psychologist or a very close friend can listen and give comfort that people may not be able to give themselves.

People who have written about their experiences before their death have given us a better understanding of what might be going on in their minds and hearts. It is not uncommon to read about people who are dying who have found their five senses coming alive. They see more clearly: the colours of autumn, the snow fall on an evergreen tree, or a flower grow over several weeks. They hear sounds of birds and leaves falling that we regularly miss. They smell fresh-baked bread, feel a cool summer night's breeze and hear the traffic noises of a busy street. They turn the stress of dying into an opportunity to live.

Others who are bedridden and nearing death feel purpose in simply receiving other people's love and prayers. These people who are dying encourage so many others to take time to talk, touch, laugh and love. They can bind a family together and leave memories that will give their loved ones great strength during a difficult time of mourning. It is a wonderful gift and a purposeful one.

CHILDREN AND DYING

This book is too short to permit a detailed account of how children view their own death or the death of a parent, grandparent or friend. Books are helpful supplements to our understanding of how children feel about death at different age levels. Very young children don't understand what death is about and therefore we need to talk to them about it. Avoiding or not exposing children to death will only make it more difficult for them to understand it later.

Children's reaction to death will depend on their intellectual and emotional maturity as well as their age level. Obviously a four year old child has different concepts of death than a ten year old child. Like adults, each child is different and will understand and accept death differently. The younger the child, the more likely she is to take our explanations literally. Imagine the image a child might have when we talk about someone who is dead as "sleeping," or that we have "lost them," or that "Daddy is in heaven looking at us," or "God has taken her away." These words are meant to comfort a child but they often frighten the child instead.

Rather, honest answers to questions of "Where is Mommy?" are better. If you have a religious belief in an afterlife, explain it clearly. If you are not sure of your own feelings say: "I'm not sure but I believe...." or "Gee, I wonder about that myself sometimes."

Children's concerns are more often about being abandoned. Will their parents die and if so, what will happen to them? They need reassurance and love rather than a quick reply not to worry. We can help our children by using the example of the death of a pet, a plant, or a news story on television to discuss feelings.

It is all right to cry with your children and to express your grief. It allows them to share their grief with you. Touching and honest talking can make a real difference. Very intense grief can be frightening to children and must be explained to them. Let them know that you have experienced death and grief before and that the hurt and pain of grieving lessen with time even though the memories of their loved one will not. Deal openly with anger, guilt and fear.

For a child who is dying, the suggestions are much the same. Children at a young age are more aware of what is going on around them than we acknowledge. When children are dying at a young age their maturity increases more rapidly. They watch and learn from their parents' and doctors' body language and they also learn from other children who are dying. They need to talk about dying just as adults do.

Check with your doctor, support groups and professional counsellors to help you and your children understand what is happening and how you can turn the months or years to follow into a memorable time. Children, even when they are dying, need the same things as all children: friends, play time, vacations, the occasional junk food, to get into trouble and to be scolded like everyone else. They need to feel normal just as an adult who is dying needs to feel normal and needed.

You will find from the books in the Recommended Readings that parents often make similar mistakes when their child is dying: spoiling the child, not talking openly enough with their child and their other children, assuming the child thinks a certain way, or trying to protect their children from the truth. When a child is dying, the child, the parents and other family members and friends need to talk about their thoughts, fears and feelings.

FAMILY AND FRIENDS

What can I do to help someone who is dying? How do I overcome my fear of saying the wrong thing? Does someone who is dying want to talk about dying? They wouldn't be interested in hearing about my job, the kids and our vacation would they? I'm scared. What do I do?

Death is a topic that few people can talk about openly except in a general philosophical sense during a card game, a fishing trip or after a news story about a terrorist act. People often find it very difficult to talk about dying when they actually know someone who is dying. It has been a social taboo to talk honestly with someone who is dying.

Most of the literature written about death and dying concentrates on the person who is dying and sometimes the family. Very little is written about what practical things you can do to help the person dying while helping yourself to feel useful.

The "right" attitude toward people who are dying is neither that of an indulgent grandmother nor of a dispassionate observer. The best that anyone can do is to care sincerely, be respectful and offer to listen.

Sometimes people say or do things that unintentionally hurt the person they care about. If their concern and caring are real then any errors they make are overshadowed by their compassion and love. There are specific things you can do to improve the life of someone who is dying but few are greater than your expression of caring. If you can openly tell the person who is dying that you, too, are afraid sometimes; that you, too, feel angry or lonely, then you open the door to honest communication. You allow the person to choose how much he wants to talk and what he wants to talk about.

One person who was dying of cancer had her friend come to visit. The friend was unable to talk about the patient's illness but did express his own fear of cancer. Some people would consider this unsympathetic. After all, the visitor wasn't dying. Yet his need to talk about cancer and his own possible death, allowed the patient to console him, offer him insight and most important, feel useful herself. Two caring people helping each other in the best way they knew how.

One of the rules we think we should follow is that when someone is sick we must talk quietly and solemnly. Others think that only a long list of bad jokes will help the person out of a slump. What is probably best is to combine many emotions together. People need to laugh, to cry, to love, to hope, to express faith but also to be angry. That is the beauty of friendship and companionship; you can listen, without judgment, and let the person express his own needs while you express yours.

Family and Friends: Visiting Someone Who is Ill Many family members and friends find it difficult to visit someone who is very ill. If the person is in the hospital, it may be more difficult for some family members and friends to visit because of some past negative experiences they had in a hospital.

It is natural to hesitate in seeing someone you love who is in pain or is seriously ill. Here are some suggestions that may help you to visit someone who is seriously ill.

1. If you care about the person then go and visit, even if you are not great friends (i.e. a colleague from work).
2. Check with the patient, the family or nurses' station to see when the best time would be to visit. You don't want 20 people arriving one day and no one coming the next.
3. Remember that the person you love has not changed. She may be your parent, your child or a dear friend. Her personality, the qualities you admire and love, have not changed because she is ill or tired. Respect her rather than baby her. Include her in decisions. Ask her advice. She will probably change less than you will.
4. There is nothing as comforting as a touch. If the person will allow you and if you feel comfortable yourself, sit close to the person, hold her hand and give her a hug. Your touch and the caring in your eyes express more than words ever can.
5. Use open-ended questions to permit the patient to decide what he wants to talk about (if he wants to talk at all). Questions like: "How are you

feeling today?" "Are you comfortable?" "I love you so much. Is there anything I can do or say that would help?"

6. Perhaps you can show or give this book to a family member or a friend to help them understand better what is happening to them and to the people around them. A small section of the book may open up the discussion in a non-threatening way. A book like this left with a person may or may not be read but it provides information to people who are naturally curious.

7. Don't prepare a speech. Admit your fear of hospitals or sick people. The patient needs to feel useful and if you are honest he can help you overcome some of your fear so that you can have a really good talk.

8. Be yourself. Act as you always do with the person. If you are naturally quiet then avoid telling all the latest jokes from work. If you normally gossip about old friends then continue to do so. If you are naturally outgoing don't become somber and serious. People need stability in their lives and family and friends can offer the greatest emotional stability.

9. Let the patients vent their anger, frustration and despair. Their feelings are real and they need to get them out. It may have nothing to do with their illness but could be their treatment, their employer's attitude, old friends who no longer visit, or an acquaintance who owes them money but is nowhere to be seen. Offer to help if you can help improve the situation.

10. It is often not helpful to compare the patient with other people who have gone through similar things. It minimizes his or her own feelings.

11. It is all right to cry and show your own feelings. You don't have to be strong all the time, for that makes the patient dependent on your strength. If you cry and allow him to be strong it is a normal relationship and one that benefits both of you.

12. Don't hide behind a gift or card for it is your presence that is the gift. You can send a card or gift if you are unable to visit, or between visits, to let the person know you are thinking of her.

13. Try not to stay too long. Two short visits are better than one long one. This is especially true if the person tires easily.

14. Remember the other family members. They need your emotional support, too, and practical things like transportation, food, baby-sitting and running errands can reduce their stress and provide them with the precious gift of time.

Family and Friends: Other Things You Can Do

Before the person dies

1. If you are a close family member or friend, offer to help with estate and funeral planning if you feel this is appropriate.

2. Encourage the person to resolve any unfinished business, including family conflicts.

3. If appropriate, help the person plan the surrounding environment i.e. have the music/food/films/videos handy that the person enjoys, arrange to

have visitors arrive in smaller numbers, move the person to a more active or comfortable room. These little things give a person a sense of control, peace and comfort.

After the person dies

1. Attend the funeral. Again a hug can mean more than standard comments like: "He lived a long life." (Not long enough for me.) "It is better this way." (Not for me!) "She would want you to be happy." (I can't be happy now.) "You did everything you could." (Maybe I did, but she is still gone and it hurts.)
2. The family will have lots of visitors for the first week or two. Plan to be there near the month anniversary. Offer to listen.
3. Do not expect the pain of losing someone dear to end after a few months. It can easily take several years before anniversaries, birthdays, songs, smells, faces in a crowd, favorite foods, found letters, clothes, photos, gifts and so many other things no longer bring tears of sorrow and loneliness. Be patient.
4. Let the grieving person talk repetitively about the person who has died. People often need to repeat over and over again the sequence of events leading to a death or repeat memories that are especially important. Talking relieves anxiety and the inner pressure to not forget the person. It makes the situation real when they wish it wasn't. Try an open-ended question to encourage such communication.
5. Do not be afraid to mention the dead person's name. People need to remember and don't want to go through life as if the person never lived. Even if the mention of the name brings tears it is a most valuable gift.
6. If you know of support groups that might help, provide the information without forcing the people to go. Information is useful and allows people to decide what needs they have. (See appendix with a list of possible support groups.)

GRIEVING

People who die continue to help the living. Not in material or mystical ways. They influenced our lives because they lived. Our thoughts and the way we view the world are influenced by the lessons and example given to us by these special people. When we have a difficult decision to make we think how they might have handled it. When we hear a certain phrase, see a particular movie or remember a certain moment, their memory continues to help us.

There is no right or wrong way to grieve except that in extreme situations, intensive grieving can injure a person physically and/or mentally. Grieving is a very personal process dependent on your cultural background and your own needs. The only predictable aspect of grieving is that it is a process you must go through to reach the end. At the end, the pain is less, the memories more positive and you are able to move forward with your own life.

To reach that end you must go through difficult and painful events such as funeral preparations, cleaning out closets, finding and reading old letters, getting through the bureaucratic paper work of settling the estate and more. Each painful event is part of the healing process.

Thoughts about Grieving Grieving is a difficult subject to write about in such a short space. In the Recommended Readings there are many books listed that deal more specifically with grieving. Here are just a few points I think are worth mentioning.

1. Feel your hurt rather than fighting it. The world feels like it is coming to an end and you share this feeling with everyone else who grieves the loss of someone important. Knowing that this debilitating sense of loss is normal and that it will become less intense over time, allows you to make it through this process as a whole person.
2. Face the reality of the death. Begin by continuing small daily activities, return to work when you feel ready, continue your relationships with people you are close to, talk about your feelings when you can.
3. Remember the good with the bad. Talk to someone about these memories. You may want to repeat over and over again what your feelings are, what memories you have that are particularly important. Find a friend to talk or write to about these feelings. Repetition is important to make your loss real. Tell her what your needs are and ask if she will help you with them.
4. If you feel the need, seek spiritual help. If you rely on books for comfort then begin to read again. If travel or work are therapeutic then do them. If you need to hide away for a few days to allow yourself to feel depressed then give yourself that time. Playing a musical instrument vigorously may also be therapeutic.
5. When you feel ready, begin to invest your emotional energy in new relationships or stronger relationships with old friends. It is not a betrayal of the person who has died or an effort to forget him. It is sharing your love again as you did with the person who has died.

Final Note: some people talk about different stages of grieving. People go through various "stages" after any loss. Whether a loved one has died, or people have lost a job or become unable to fulfill a dream, their reactions are surprisingly alike; the degree of the reaction will be different. Stages only help you label feelings and shouldn't be considered a rule to follow in your grief.

People who are dying may experience different emotions or they may keep denying their illness to the end. People who are grieving may do the same by denying their need to experience grief. At the same time, not all of their anger or depression is caused by their grief. Their life continues and so do their normal frustrations with plumbing, rude automobile drivers, and job tensions. If you understand whether your own feelings are from grief or from normal living you will be able to accept the reality of your situation and deal with your stresses more realistically.

CAREGIVER STRESSES

Much of what I have written about helping the patient and family members during a person's illness, and the grieving afterward, holds true for caregivers as well. Caregivers are human beings first and some people affect them more visibly than others. When my mother died, our family physician, the visiting nurse and the homemaker sat together and cried. They did not pretend to be strong, they did not worry about embarrassment and most importantly, they did not go away. They stayed and expressed their feelings honestly. It was their greatest gift to the rest of my family for it showed us their concern without words.

Palliative/hospice care bereavement programs follow many of these suggestions by allowing people to express their feelings, keep in contact with some of the caregivers, and use the sense of touch to express concern.

When we look at caregiver stress, I will separate caregivers who work in palliative/hospice care from acute care doctors, nurses, therapists, clerics, psychologists and the others.

Acute Care Caregivers These people may have the following stresses:
1. difficulty in accepting that a patient's physical and psychosocial problems cannot always be controlled;
2. difficulty in deciding how much to tell a patient about her condition;
3. the severe constraints of time involved in patient care, administrative responsibilities, family concerns, and professional development;
4. frustration at being involved with a patient's family whose emotional resources have already been drained by the patient's illness;
5. disappointment at being unable to fulfill patient/family's expectation of dying a good death;
6. anger at being critically reviewed by the public;
7. difficulty in deciding how involved to get with the patient and the family especially outside of normal working hours;
8. frustration in their inability to give the kind of care they want to give.

Palliative/Hospice Caregivers The stresses of palliative/hospice caregivers differ from those of acute care staff. Their professional position has been given less credibility because they are dealing with people who are dying. There are no miracle cures and there is an erroneous assumption that their work is, therefore, less rewarding or valuable.

The philosophy of physical, emotional and spiritual support is not always easy to fulfill. Some patients have not accepted their situation. Some patients and families have major unresolved problems that frustrate the caregivers' hope for a peaceful and comforting death for a patient.

The relative newness of palliative/hospice care means that the systems have not been perfected to everyone's satisfaction and people's egos in designing the program, according to what they think is best, creates friction with other well-meaning caregivers.

Caregivers grieve someone's death in their own individual way. In cases where they have come to know patients and their families closely, the grieving is more acute. There are few people outside of hospice care who can understand the mixture of personal satisfaction and professional stresses that these caregivers have. One of the advantages of working in hospice care is that professional stresses are more clearly identified and addressed. The following list describes some of the differences between acute care and hospice care personnel.

1. There may be less conflict regarding a patient's death because hospice care is concerned with comfort rather than prolonging life.
2. There is a lower patient/caregiver ratio in hospice care so that time and administrative stresses are reduced.
3. There is a team spirit in hospice care and an acceptance of the hospice care philosophy that gives a different direction and purpose than that found in modern acute care facilities.
4. There is more open and honest communication between caregivers and the patient/family which decreases the need for medical secrecy.
5. There is great patient/family satisfaction and approval of hospice care teams which reflects well on the caregivers.
6. There is often specialized training for hospice caregivers which prepares them for their work.
7. There are fewer acute or unpredicatable situations. There are also fewer concerns about lawsuits since patients, families and caregivers are working together with a more predictable illness toward an understood end.

Dr. Stephen Fleming, an Associate Professor at York University, states that the nature of the hospice care philosophy encourages team meetings to discuss issues, concerns and feelings. A psychologist or psychiatrist may come in regularly to discuss staff concerns individually or at a group meeting. Patient rounds help the caregivers to review each patient and family on a daily basis. The hospice care philosophy promotes a combined effort of the caregivers and a system of informed decision making. The staff feels part of a team. Patient and family satisfaction encourages improved care and a sense of personal satisfaction for the caregivers.

LETTERS WRITTEN TO FAMILY, FRIENDS AND COLLEAGUES

One of the very special gifts someone who is dying can give to her or his family, friends and colleagues is to write a note or letter to them. It could be read before or after the death.

You know all too well the stress and grief that your family and friends will have when you die. You also know how cherished a note or letter would be as a gift to them. Words of encouragement, understanding, friendship and love would help them through a difficult time of grieving.

For those of you with children a letter, cassette or video tape filled with your love, your thoughts, your hopes and dreams for your children would be a life-long expression of parental faith and love. These will not be easy to do, especially for those very close to you. You do not need to write a long letter or a diary. My mother gave my father a book of Norman Rockwell prints and signed it: "All my love." It said it all perfectly. It was the last thing she wrote.

When my father was dying, he had my sister write out numerous cards for him which he signed. It was a goodbye to his family and friends. It drained him but he wanted people to know he was thinking of them; just as they were thinking of him. He asked my sister to write a special wedding card for my fiancee and me. On my wedding day it brought tears of sadness, tears of joy and great love and pride. A very special gift shared between my father, my sister, my wife and myself.

CHAPTER TWELVE

PREPARING LEGAL AND FINANCIAL AFFAIRS

Preparing a Legal Will
Organ Donation
Financial Planning
Personal Information Record
Documents and Property Checklist
Personal Financial Status

PREPARING A LEGAL WILL

Each jurisdiction in Canada and the United States has regulations regarding the disposition of a person's estate after death and what type of wills are acceptable.

In Canada, for example, most provinces permit the use of an unwitnessed handwritten will, while British Columbia requires a typed will witnessed by two people.

The purpose of the will is very simple. It states what you wish done with your assets; who gets what and how much. It may also include funeral instructions, your request that a family member or friend be the guardian of your children, and sometimes a last word to specific family members and friends.

Some jurisdictions limit the power of your will. For example, a jurisdiction may have regulations requiring division of the estate to include former spouses and dependent children by a former marriage. Your request to leave your children under the care of another family member or friend may not be followed in some jurisdictions where it is up to the court to determine who can best care for the children.

It is important to realize that each jurisdiction has its own regulations regarding wills and the disposition of estates therefore you should get professional advice to ensure that your wishes are followed as much as possible and that estate taxes are kept to a minimum.

Every adult member of a family should have a will and have it renewed at least every five years. A new will is often legally required after a marriage or divorce.

ORGAN DONATION

Most legislative jurisdictions have their own Anatomical Gift Act. Check your local laws to ensure that your wishes will be carried out properly.

Some general information about organ/body donations:

- many medical schools have sufficient bodies for study but some schools still require donations;
- transportation costs are generally not paid for by medical schools;
- the body can be present for funeral or memorial services whether an organ or the whole body is donated;
- the ideal people for organ and body donation are less than 60 years old. Their weight is not a factor but generally cancer patients (except in some cases of brain cancer) are not acceptable for organ donations.
- the common organ transplants are: skin, heart, liver, kidney, lung, cornea, pancreas, certain bones, middle ear;
- the time factor is crucial in most organ transplants, therefore, hospital deaths are most suitable for transplants except for cornea and skin transplants;
- some organs (eye, skin and some bones) may be suitable for "banking" for up to 48 hours.
- organ or body donations do not have to be accepted by a medical team so make alternative plans;
- there are many organizations in North America which coordinate organ donation. Donor cards may be part of a driver's license, or you can become of a member of an international organization such as the Living Bank. Check what is available in your local area or write to one of the organizations listed in the Appendix.

FINANCIAL PLANNING

Financial planning can help your executor/executrix and family administer your estate. There are many tax and legal considerations. In some cases it may be wise to transfer bank accounts and other assets before your death to save on possible inheritance taxes and probate costs.

You or a family member should check with your local government regarding legal and tax considerations regarding your estate. If your estate is somewhat complex, or if you have real estate and other major investments, it would be wise to get the advice of an accountant and/or lawyer.

The "Financial Status" form in this chapter will help you record your financial affairs. Again, you or a family member, friend or accountant should fill out these forms to help you understand the extent of your estate. Many people who say they have nothing may be amazed at the effect these inflationary times have had on their net worth.

I suggest you use a black pen to fill in those sections of the forms that will not change (e.g. names, past events). For information that will change (e.g. financial data, addresses), use a dark pencil. Read all of the sections within a form first *before* writing in any information. This will familiarize you with the forms and prevent you from repeating information within the same form.

You might consider signing a Power of Attorney to give a family member, friend, lawyer or accountant the power to handle your financial affairs at times when you are unable to. This would permit someone to do your banking, pay your bills, look after your investments and discover ways to minimize any taxes or probate costs.

A Power of Attorney, easily drawn up in most jurisdictions, simply states that you give a named person the right to handle your financial affairs and that the Power of Attorney can be revoked at any time. It should be witnessed and, in certain circumstances, notarized to ensure that you are signing away these rights voluntarily.

PERSONAL INFORMATION RECORD

1. Full legal name: _____

2. Previous surname if applicable: _____

3. Sex: _____

4. Telephone: _____
                       Daytime   Evening

5. Legal residence address: _____

_____

6. Mailing address if different: _____

_____

7. Year you began residence: _____

8. Other residences: (e.g. summer home) _____

_____

9. Work address: _____

_____

10. Social Insurance Number (Canadian): _____

11. Social Security Number (USA): _____

12. Date of birth: _____

13. Place of birth: _____

14. Marital status (circle answer):   single,   married,   widowed, or   divorced.

15. If married or widowed give person's full name, including any previous surname: (if more than one, use a separate page)

_____

16. Date and place of marriage: _____

_____

17. If widowed give date and place of death: _____

_____

PERSONAL INFORMATION RECORD (continued)

18. If previously married give name of former spouse(s) and date(s) marriage ended:

_____   _____

_____   _____

_____   _____

_____   _____

19. Father's full legal name: _____

20. Birthdate and birthplace: _____

21. Address and phone number if still living: _____

_____

22. Mother's full legal (Maiden) name: _____

23. Birthdate and birthplace: _____

24. Address and phone number if still living: _____

_____

25. Your Nationality: _____

26. If nationality has changed give previous nationality: _____

27. Occupation: _____

28. Employer name and address: _____

_____

29. Religious affiliation (including name of your cleric and place of worship):

_____

_____

30. Important dates and locations of significant religious ceremonies (e.g. baptism, confirmation, bar mitzvah):

_____

_____

_____

_____

PERSONAL INFORMATION RECORD (continued)

31. If you were a veteran:

a) date and place of enlistment: _____

b) date and place of discharge: _____

c) service number: _____

d) organization or outfit: _____

e) rank or rating: _____

f) commendations received: _____

_____

g) location of discharge papers: _____

h) would you like flag to drape casket?: _____

32. Name, address, telephone and relationship of my expected survivors (or give location of where these addresses can be found e.g. your address book):

Name:	Address:	Phone:	Relationship:

PERSONAL INFORMATION RECORD (continued)

33. Name, address, telephone and relationship of important relatives and friends (or give location of where these addresses can be found):

Name:	Address:	Phone:	Relationship:

34. Executor/Executrix (name): _____

Address: _____

_____

Telephone: _____
        Daytime   Evening

35. Family physician (name): _____

Address: _____

_____

Telephone: _____

PERSONAL INFORMATION RECORD (continued)

36. Lawyer (name): _____

Address: _____

_____

Telephone: _____

37. Accountant (name): _____

Address: _____

_____

Telephone: _____

DOCUMENTS AND PROPERTY CHECKLIST

Documents

Name	Registration No. (where applicable)	Location
1. Passport no.	_____	_____
2. Medical Insurance no.	_____	_____
3. Driver's license	_____	_____
4. Birth Certificate	_____	_____
5. Marriage Certificate(s)	_____	_____
6. Separation/Divorce Papers	_____	_____
7. Children's Birth Certificate(s)	_____	_____
8. Last Will and Testament	_____	_____
9. Living Will	_____	_____
10. Power of Attorney	_____	_____
11. Military Discharge	_____	_____
12. Income Tax Records	_____	_____
13. Mortgages and Notes	_____	_____
14. Deeds and Titles	_____	_____
15. Address book	_____	_____
16. Other Documents:	_____	_____
_____	_____	_____
_____	_____	_____
_____	_____	_____

17. Credit Card Name	No.	Expiry Date
_____	_____	__/__
_____	_____	__/__
_____	_____	__/__
_____	_____	__/__
_____	_____	__/__
_____	_____	__/__

Property

17. Safety Deposit Box(es):

a) Located: _____

b) Box number: _____

c) Key number: _____

d) Key location: _____

18. Principal Financial Institution: (e.g. bank)

_____

Address: _____

_____

Telephone: _____

Type of account(s): _____

Account number(s): _____

19. Secondary Financial Institution: (e.g. trust company)

_____

Address: _____

_____

Telephone: _____

Type of account(s): _____

Account number(s): _____

20. Location of Bank Books, Records: _____

21. Insurance policies: (if more than one, use a separate page)

Name of company: _____

Address: _____

_____

Telephone: _____

Type of insurance(s): _____

Insurance Policy number(s): _____

Name of insured: _____

Beneficiary: _____

Agent's name: _____

Address: _____

_____

Telephone: _____

22. Location of policy(ies): _____

23. Real Estate: (if more than one property, use separate page) Location: _____

Assessed value: $ _____

Mortgage(s): $ _____

Mortgaged with: _____

Mortgage number: _____

Name on Deed Title: _____

Property insured with: _____

Address: _____

_____

Telephone: _____

Agent's name: _____

Address: _____

_____

Telephone: _____

Policy number and amount: _____

24. Home contents insured with: _____

Agent's name: _____

Address: _____

_____

Telephone: _____

Policy number and amount: _____

25. Government Bonds: _____

Value: $ _____

Located: _____

26. Corporation Bonds: _____

Value: $ _____

Located: _____

27. Guaranteed Investments: _____

Value: $ _____

28. Stocks, Shares and other Securities (if you require more space, use a separate page):

Company	Type & Number of Shares
_____	_____
_____	_____
_____	_____
_____	_____
_____	_____
_____	_____
_____	_____
_____	_____
_____	_____
_____	_____
_____	_____
_____	_____

Family Heirlooms

Name	Location

29. Furniture: (list)

_____   _____

_____   _____

_____   _____

_____   _____

30. Wedding Ring(s):

_____   _____

31. Jewelry/Medals: (list)

_____   _____

_____   _____

_____   _____

32. Photos:

_____   _____

33. Old letters:

_____   _____

34. Diaries:

_____   _____

35. Cassette tapes:

_____   _____

36. Home movies/videos:

_____   _____

37. Career papers/awards: (list)

_____   _____

_____   _____

_____   _____

38. Family tree:

_____   _____

_____   _____

39. Books: (list)

_____   _____

_____   _____

_____   _____

_____   _____

_____   _____

_____   _____

_____   _____

_____   _____

PERSONAL FINANCIAL STATUS

(To be completed before death if possible, and reviewed by the executor/executrix after death. For each major section below e.g. retirement savings or bank loans, make a separate itemized list. For estates more complicated than this form can accommodate, I suggest you get the advice of an estate accountant and ask him or her to prepare your financial records and provide you with photocopies.)

Estimated Assets

1. Cash: _____

2. Insurance policies: _____

3. Retirement savings: _____

4. Business interests: _____

5. Total Securities: _____

6. Money owed by others: _____

7. Real Estate: _____

8. Pensions: _____

9. Annuities: _____

10. Trusts: _____

11. Household effects: _____

12. Cars: _____

13. Boat, snowmobile, & others: _____

14. Collections (coins, art, etc.): _____

15. Other assets: (list) _____

_____   _____

_____   _____

_____   _____

_____   _____

_____   _____

    Total Estimated Assets: _____

As of this date: _____

Estimated Liabilities

1. Mortgages: _____

2. Real estate contracts: _____

3. Bank loans: _____

4. Personal loans: _____

5. Credit card, charge accounts: _____

6. Personal bills (telephone, gas, hydro, T.V.): _____

7. Pending lawsuits: _____

8. Unsettled claims: _____

9. Outstanding taxes: _____

10. Back alimony and child support: _____

11. Other debts: (list)

_____ _____

_____ _____

_____ _____

_____ _____

_____ _____

Total Liabilities: _____

As of this date: _____

Note: if you have liabilities that your family doesn't know about (i.e. gambling or personal business debts,) keep a record with your lawyer, executor or friend. Otherwise your next of kin could be emotionally and financially hurt after your death.

CHAPTER THIRTEEN

PREPARING FUNERAL ARRANGEMENTS

Definitions of Funeral Terms
Questions Regarding Conventional Funerals
Disposition of the Body
Questions Regarding Cemeteries
Questions Regarding Cremation
Arrangements for Monuments and Markers
Funeral and Cemetery Service Instructions
Checklist for Survivors

Pre-planning a funeral and the disposition of the body (i.e. burial, cremation or donation) can save a lot of emotional strain for survivors. After a death, the survivors have limited physical and emotional energy so advanced planning will not only save money but it will also help the remaining family. If possible shop around for the kind of service you want at the most reasonable costs. It would be a serious mistake to leave the arrangements for such major investments till the last minute. If the funeral and disposition of the body have not been pre-planned, use the forms at the end of this chapter to help you make some of the decisions.

The first rule of planning a funeral service is not to feel rushed. If a person has died at a hospital there is no need to rush him or her to a funeral home. The hospital has facilities to keep the body for a time to let family members or friends make the proper arrangements.

There are basically two types of general funeral services available to the public:

1. traditional funeral services and;
2. services arranged through a Memorial Society at reduced costs.

Neither service is better than the other. Just as some people prefer large weddings over smaller, less expensive weddings, there are others who prefer more elaborate funerals over less expensive ones.

Let us begin with some definitions of terms used by funeral professionals to help you understand the choices available to you.

DEFINITIONS OF FUNERAL TERMS

Conventional Funerals: funerals organized through a licensed funeral home at an average 1985 cost of $2,500.00 in the U.S. and $2,600.00 in Canada. This figure does not include costs related to cemeteries, flowers, or headstones/monuments. Funeral service establishments and funeral directors must be licensed in all U.S. states except Colorado and in all Canadian provinces except British Columbia (licensing in B.C. is expected in the near future).

Memorial Society Funerals: Memorial Societies are non-profit, non-sectarian consumer organizations that deal directly with select funeral homes to promote simple and dignified funerals at reduced costs. For a nominal fee (i.e. $10.00-20.00) members of these societies receive the latest information on low-cost yet dignified funerals. These societies also act as consumer watchdogs on legislation regarding funerals. They do not arrange funerals themselves.

Non-professional Funeral: a funeral arranged privately without the assistance of a funeral home. The family or friends prepare and transport the body, provide the casket and obtain the legal documents. This option requires the family or friends to understand the local laws to insure no violations are made. The family physician or a cemetery official may be able to provide the information regarding legal requirements. This process involves a considerable effort for people not accustomed to these procedures but it is possible.

Funeral Director: also called a Mortician (avoid the title Undertaker as it is disliked by most funeral directors). Funeral Directors must be licensed, except in Colorado and British Columbia, to provide funeral services.

Funeral: usually implies that the body is present for post-death services. A funeral usually includes a religious ceremony in a place of worship or in the funeral home chapel. The funeral may be preceded by a "wake" or "visitation" where people can pay their respects to the deceased and immediate family. The casket may be open or closed.

Memorial Service: usually implies that the body is not present for any post-death services. This service may be held in a place of worship, funeral home chapel, at someone's home or another location. (Not to be confused with a Memorial Society Funeral.)

Body Donation: although people may donate their body to a medical school, the school is not obligated to accept the donation. It is important to make such arrangements before death and have an alternative method of body disposition.

Funeral Costs: Memorial Societies have set fees in agreement with specific funeral homes. The various "plans" encourage low-cost caskets, few extra services such as visitations, no embalming etc. Conventional funerals vary greatly in price as each funeral is based on service-used fees. Some of the services that are available (but not always necessary) in either case include: removal of the body from place of death; the care and preparation of the body (embalming is optional in most cases); coordination between family and clergy for religious service; preparation and filing legal documents; preparation of the obituary; use of facilities and equipment; use of the chapel; visitations; the casket; and transportation to the cemetery or crematorium.

Other Costs: the clerics; use of the place of worship; organist; flowers; transportation of the body from another town/city; and burial or crematorium charges. In cases of body donation to a medical school, the cost of transportation and other costs may be involved.

Embalming: the disinfection of the body by replacing body fluids with chemicals. Prevents quick deterioration of the body and the odors that accompany deterioration. Generally not required except in certain circumstances, e.g., if the body is to be transported between states/provinces. Embalming does not preserve the body indefinitely.

Pre-planning: saves the survivors many decisions but should provide flexibility for them to change parts of the plan to meet unexpected circumstances. Memorial Societies and some funeral homes encourage pre-arranging your funerals and disposition of bodies. They keep a record of your wishes on file and will transfer the file to any area in the country you move to.

Pre-financing: for funerals, burials and cremations can permit you to pay today's prices for tomorrow's services. Be sure that your funds are put in trust and cannot be used for any purpose other than the services you have paid for. Determine whether you can withdraw your funds (ask if there is an administrative fee charged), or transfer them to another funeral home or cemetery, should you wish to do so at a later date. Ask for a detailed list of services and costs before agreeing to purchase anything. Try to include other members of the family in the decisions.

QUESTIONS REGARDING CONVENTIONAL FUNERALS

1. Is the funeral home and funeral director licensed? (Except in Colorado and British Columbia, all reputable funeral homes and directors must be licensed.)
2. Will the funeral home provide a written memorandum of the decisions you have made including all direct and indirect costs?
3. If you are pre-arranging and pre-financing your own funeral will the funeral home keep your funds in trust? Can you withdraw or transfer your funds and if so at what cost?
4. If the funeral has been pre-financed will the funds cover all direct and indirect costs at the time of death?
5. What complaint system is in force in cases of disagreement on services and costs?
6. If you have selected a Memorial Society-style funeral, will the funeral home accept it and at Memorial Society costs?

DISPOSITION OF THE BODY

Just as funerals can be quite expensive, the disposition of the body can also be expensive. Again, pre-planning can save the survivors' physical and emotional energy. However, if you know what you want and how to get it, disposition of the body does not have to be difficult.

Earth Burial/Internment: burial can be in a municipal, church, veteran or other non-profit cemetery, or in a privately-owned fraternal or corporate cemetery. Provincial/State jurisdictions may regulate cemeteries including whether they must have an endowment or perpetual care fund to ensure that the cemetery grounds and individual graves are properly maintained. A point to remember is that some cemeteries are non-profit and others are owned for profit. Prices do not vary greatly but services offered and care provided may be different.

Cremation: is a process of combustion and evaporation that reduces human remains to bone fragments. These cremated remains may be stored in a container (urn) and kept anywhere you wish or buried in a cemetery plot or placed in a columbarium. Cremated remains are sometimes scattered but local laws should be checked to ensure the legality of scattering. NOTE: some religions do not permit some of these practices. Check with your cleric or funeral director.

Entombment: the casket is placed into a mausoleum crypt (above-ground structure) and sealed by a marble or granite face. Mausoleums are usually on the cemetery grounds.

Vault or Lawn Crypt: a concrete box in the ground where a casket is placed and then sealed with a lid. This prevents the ground from caving in around the casket. Elaborate vaults are available.

Columbarium: a structure where urns of cremated remains are placed into one of many spaces or niches. This structure may be part of a mausoleum.

Headstones/Monuments: some cemeteries will have limits regarding the size, shape, material used (granite versus concrete) or whether the marker must be flush with the ground or stand up.

Traditional Cemetery versus Memorial Park/Garden: traditional cemeteries permit upright monuments, usually made of stone. Memorial Parks/Gardens have existed for about 60 years and have bronze or granite memorials level with the ground to blend in with the landscape of lawns, trees, flowers and gardens. Either can be publicly or privately owned, for profit or non-profit.

Pre-planning: does not involve a cost reduction (considered unfair business practice) but does permit shopping around, making a choice you prefer regarding location, services and costs, avoiding estate problems and giving peace of mind. Many cemeteries permit you to withdraw your pre-paid funds with little or no charge. Cemeteries may also belong to the National Exchange Trust which will credit your account to another cemetery elsewhere in the country.

Relationship with Funeral Homes: in some jurisdictions funeral homes own their own cemetery which may mean a cost reduction. When the cemetery is not affiliated with a funeral home, it is best to go to the cemetery yourself to make your own choices because in most cases, the cemetery staff will have more information available than the funeral home staff.

QUESTIONS REGARDING CEMETERIES

1. Is this cemetery or memorial park/garden licensed?

    a. With which authority?

    b. Who owns this cemetery or memorial park/garden, and

    c. how long has it been in existence?

2. According to local laws how many days do I have to cancel this agreement without penalty? (Check with your local government agency, Better Business Bureau or consumer organization to make sure you are getting what you pay for.)

3. What is the size of the plots available?

4. Do you have any restrictions regarding the type of monument or marker I wish to use?

    a. Can I buy one separately or must I buy one from the cemetery?

5. Does the marker or monument have to be made out of granite or bronze? (Granite and bronze last longest.)

6. Are there any restrictions on religious or cultural observances, such as not being able to use lighted candles at the grave or having a survivor sit with a chair on the plot?

7. Can you supply me with a list of the various options and services available plus their costs, i.e. burial, a crypt in a mausoleum, a niche, opening and closing the grave/crypt, and installing a memorial?

8. Can I pre-pay through time-payments?

9. Do you have a perpetual care fund so that I will not have to pay maintenance costs each year?

10. Can I cancel any pre-arranged plans and get back any pre-paid funds?

    a. Are there any administrative penalties for this service?

11. Can I transfer my pre-arranged plan and pre-paid funds to another cemetery or memorial park/garden?

12. Are you a member of the National Exchange Trust or similar organization?

     a. Is this cemetery or memorial park/garden a member of any local, regional or national associations? If so, which ones?

     b. What Code of Ethics or Creed of Ideals do you abide by?

13. Can you service some of our preferences which may be different from other people? e.g.

     a. planting a small garden on the plot _____

     b. _____

     c. _____

     d. _____

QUESTIONS REGARDING CREMATION

Cremations may be arranged through a funeral home or cemetery or separate company depending on local regulations.

1. How long after death can cremation occur? (Time limit is set to prevent cremation in cases when the cause of death is uncertain.)

2. Must we have a casket for cremation?

3. What local regulations are there regarding scattering of cremated remains?

4. Can you provide me with a list of options and services you offer plus a complete list of direct and indirect costs?

ARRANGEMENTS FOR MONUMENTS AND MARKERS

It is important to consider what type of monument you wish to purchase before you buy a cemetery plot. Cemeteries may restrict the kind of monuments placed on plots in different areas on the grounds so it is important to know what you want before committing to a specific plot.

You may buy a monument or marker through a special dealership or perhaps the cemetery itself. Make sure you are dealing with a reputable group and that all direct and indirect costs are made clear. Also make sure that any monument or marker you buy meets the regulations of the cemetery or memorial park/garden.

FUNERAL AND CEMETERY SERVICE INSTRUCTIONS

1. Have you pre-arranged your funeral? If yes, is it with a funeral director or memorial society?

    a. Name: _____

    b. Address: _____

                  _____

    c. Telephone: _____

    d. Contact person: _____

    e. Location of contract: _____

2. Have you purchased a cemetery plot? If yes,

    a. Where: _____

    b. Name: _____

    c. Address: _____

                  _____

    d. Telephone: _____

    e. Plot number and site: _____

    f. Location of contract: _____

3. Are you a member of a Memorial Society? If yes,

    a. Name: _____

    b. Address: _____

                  _____

    c. Telephone: _____

    d. Contact person: _____

If you have not pre-arranged your funeral and the disposition of your body, answer the following questions. If you have made arrangements, read the following questions and fill in any of your wishes that may not be recorded elsewhere.

1. Do you wish your body to be embalmed? _____

2. Do you wish to be buried or cremated? _____

3. Do you have a preference for a particular funeral home? If yes,

    a. Name: _____

    b. Address: _____

                  _____

   c. Telephone: _____

   d. Contact person: _____

4. Clothes you wish used: _____

_____

5. Jewelry you wish used: _____

_____

6. Religious items to be included in coffin (e.g. rosary): _____

_____

7. What type of casket would you like: wood, fiberglass, metal?

_____

8. Do you have a color preference for the inside and outside of the casket?

_____

9. Do you wish an open or closed casket? _____

10. If you are a veteran and entitled to a flag draped casket, is it your wish that the appropriate authorities be notified?

_____

11. Do you wish visitation rights for your family and friends? If yes,

   a. How often? _____

12. Would you like your cleric (e.g. minister, rabbi, priest) to officiate at a funeral service? If yes,

   a. Name: _____

   b. Address: _____

   c. Telephone: _____

   d. Contact person: _____

13. Would you like a funeral service in your own place of worship or would you prefer to use the funeral chapel?

_____

14. Do you have any preferences for pallbearers? If yes,

   a. Name: _____

   b. Name: _____

    c. Name: _____

    d. Name: _____

    e. Name: _____

    f. Name: _____

15. Do you wish an organist? If yes, do you have a favorite piece(s) you wish played? _____

_____

16. Do you wish a soloist or choir? If yes, do you have a favorite song(s) you wish sung? _____

_____

17. Do you have a favorite passage(s) you wish read during the service?

_____

_____

18. Do you wish flowers or do you prefer donations to your favorite charity? If a charity, which one(s): _____

_____

Disposition of the Body:

1. Are you donating your whole body immediately after death? _____

    a. Are you donating any part of your body upon death? If yes, which parts: _____

    _____

    b. Have you filled out an organ donor card? If yes,

        i. Card location: _____

        ii. Contact person's name: _____

        iii. Address: _____

        _____

        iv. Telephone: _____

        v. (If you do not have a card, please arrange to sign one and keep a copy in your wallet.)

2. Do you wish to be buried or cremated? _____

For Burials

1. Do you have a cemetery preference? If yes,

    a. Name: _____

    b. Address: _____

    _____

    c. Telephone: _____

2. What type of grave monument or marker do you wish? (i.e. stand-up monument, flat marker level with ground, plaque)

    _____

3. Do have a preferred inscription? If yes,

    a. What is it? _____

    _____

    _____

    _____

For Cremations

1. Do you have a crematorium preference? If yes,

    a. Name: _____

    b. Address: _____

    _____

    c. Telephone: _____

2. Do you wish the ashes deposited in a mausoleum or buried?

    _____

3. Do you wish the ashes given to a specific person? If yes,

    a. Name: _____

    b. Address: _____

    _____

    c. Telephone: _____

4. Do you wish the ashes scattered? If yes,

    a. By whom: _____

    b. Where: _____

(Make sure that your wish to scatter the ashes does not go against any local laws.)

Obituaries

1. Do you wish a newspaper obituary notice? If yes, name of newspaper(s): _____

_____

2. Is there anything you particularily want mentioned in your obituary:

_____

_____

_____

_____

_____

3. If you are a citizen or past citizen of another country do you wish that country's embassy to be notified of your death?

    a. If yes, name of Country Embassy: _____

    b. Address: _____

_____

    c. Telephone: _____

4. Other special instructions or information not covered by this checklist:

_____

_____

_____

_____

_____

CHECKLIST FOR SURVIVORS

Sometimes it is helpful to have a checklist of things that need to be done upon the death of a loved one. It gives you direction at a time when decisions are expected from you. Sit down with your family and divide the various tasks so that no one is overly burdened. If the executor of the estate is someone other than a family member, then you may leave many of the legal, financial, tax and bureaucratic requirements for him to complete.

The forms included in this chapter will provide you with much of the information that is required by a funeral home, executor, lawyer, family physician etc. If there was no time to fill in these forms, some of the following suggestions will help insure that everything is covered.

1. If you are alone at the time of death call someone immediately to give you emotional support and to help arrange the next few days' activities.

2. Collect the various information forms included in this book so that you do not have to provide all the information verbally.

3. Arrange for family members and friends to take turns answering the door and phone.

4. Call your funeral home to arrange for the transportation of the body to the home, and to make an appointment to finalize the arrangments. If the deceased left specific instructions, then arrange to follow them as completely as possible. If there were no instructions, decide on the type of funeral you wish and whether the body will be buried or cremated.

5. If you are not the executor/executrix then notify him/her immediately and ask for his/her assistance.

6. Decide whether you wish flowers and/or donations to a charity (assuming you have no instructions from the deceased person).

7. Make a list of the immediate family, friends and colleagues from work you want to notify by phone or telegram. Decide if you wish specific people to act as pallbearers and put a check-mark beside their name on this list.

8. You or someone else should call or telegram the people on the list to notify them of the death.

9. Make a separate list for people who live far away and whom you wish notified by letter and/or printed notice.

10. Prepare a copy of a printed notice if you wish to use one.

11. Different religions require different arrangements. For example, Roman Catholics usually use Prayer Cards at the funeral service, therefore have them printed. Your church or funeral home can suggest a printer who will

do these quickly. Other religions require other specific things to be done, so check with your cleric or funeral director for assistance.

12. If small children belonging to the deceased or to a survivor are not attending the funeral, arrange for help which will last until after the services.

13. Coordinate the supply of food for the next few days.

14. Arrange for assistance with daily household chores.

15. If people are coming from out-of-town, arrange a place for them to stay and eat.

16. Arrange for the care of any family pets.

17. Take precautions during the funeral services to protect the home against burglaries. Have someone house-sit.

18. Write an obituary. Funeral directors can offer suggestions but some or all of the following can be included: name, age, place of birth, cause of death, occupation, educational background, military service, memberships held, volunteer work, and list of the immediate family. Give the date, time and place of services. If the funeral director does not provide this service you can deliver or call in the notification of death. Some newspapers charge for this notice.

19. Plan for the disposition of the flowers after the funeral.

20. Arrange to pay the clerics, organist, and others who need payment the day of the funeral.

After the Funeral/Memorial Service

The paper work and bureaucracy of dying, the insurance policies, the probating of the will, etc. can be extremely frustrating. Whether you are the executor/executrix of the will or helping someone who is, it is important to expect delay, frustration and illogical procedures. Except for step 15, all of the following steps are usually cared out by the executor of the will. If this person is not a member of the family, he will need information and assistance from the next-of-kin during some of the steps.

1. Whenever getting information from any officials, take notes of their name, the date you spoke with them and what they said. This is especially true with large bureaucracies where each person may give you different information.

2. If the deceased lived alone, notify the utilities and post office. Have mail forwarded to your address or the executor/executrix' address.

3. If the deceased rented his home, notify the landlord and arrange a time when you can move all the belongings.

4. Get several copies of the death certificate.

5. Fill in the person's financial status form as at the time of death.

6. Notify insurance company(ies) regarding all appropriate policies.

7. Check with your local government office regarding any death benefits, military benefits, spouse/family benefits. Check with a number of sources because some programs are not widely known. Ask what specific documents you will require to get these benefits.

8. Check with credit unions, trade unions, fraternities, credit card companies, auto clubs, special associations or organizations that the deceased was a member of, for similar pensions and additional benefits.

9. Collect all outstanding bills and pay them accordingly. In cases of large bills, mortgage payments, business debts etc. you should get the advice of a lawyer and/or accountant.

10. Cancel all credit cards immediately.

11. Notify the following organizations of the person's death: driver's license bureau, charitable organizations the person contributed to, post office, pension/government health insurance and other government agencies, and organizations or associations that the person was a member of.

12. Different jurisdictions have different regulations regarding how to probate a will (if it is necessary at all!). Check with your local government to see what the regulations are. For simple estates, it is often possible to settle the will out of court without the help of a lawyer, however, family reform laws are becoming more popular, resulting in further restrictions to estate settlement. When in doubt, speak with a lawyer. You may also ask your insurance agent, funeral home director or other professionals who deal daily with these questions and who may be able to advise you or refer you to an estate lawyer.

13. Complete the person's income tax form at the end of the year. If the estate is large or complicated, with real estate holdings and numerous assets, get the advice of an accountant or tax lawyer.

14. Distribute the assets according to the person's will and auction off other assets as required. Large estates do require certain laws to be followed and again you should get legal advice on the proper procedures.

15. Make a list of people you wish to send Thank You Notes to such as those who attended the funeral, family members and friends who have sent

condolences, and physicians and other caregivers who gave the deceased and family good care.

Note: I began by saying that this process can be very frustrating and emotionally draining. It is important to recognize that the grieving process continues and that these steps are often an important part of that grieving. Cleaning out closets, selling furniture, closing bank accounts are all emotionally traumatic and will take their toll on you but they will also help you release some of the emotional pain survivors need to go through. Recognize your personal needs and ask for people's help and take time to pamper yourself. You deserve it.

Take the time you need, ASK for the help you deserve from other family members and friends (for they may not know how to offer assistance) and use this opportunity to acknowledge your real loss.

FURTHER PERSONAL NOTES

CREATING A SUPPORT TEAM

June Callwood's book Twelve Weeks in Spring tells the story of Margaret Frazer. In 1985 Margaret was dying of cancer and did not want to go into hospital or become involved in a formal palliative care program. June Callwood and other friends recruited close to 60 friends, acquaintances from Margaret's volunteer work, church, and other volunteers to help her stay at home until her death. They provided practical help as well as physical and emotional comforts. Margaret's doctor was part of this "support team" and provided the others with information to help Margaret stay as comfortable as possible. Near the end of Margaret's life this support team provided round-the-clock care and support.

From that experience several of Margaret's friends from the church of the Holy Trinity and other volunteers established Trinity Hospice Toronto to help people who wanted to keep as much control over their lives as possible through an informal hospice program. The volunteers at Trinity Hospice Toronto provide practical care and supports during 1-3 hour visits with someone who has a terminal or life-threatening illness. These volunteers are not trained medical staff (although some volunteers have professional backgrounds) nor is their purpose to replace homecare and homemaker supports available through government health care. Their purpose is to provide the kind of practical help and emotional support that friends and good neighbours have been providing for each other for generations.

I spoke with Trinity Hospice Toronto's Beth Pelton (Co-ordinator) and Elaine Hall (Resource Person) about how people could design their own support teams to allow them the most control and flexibility at a time when they had a terminal or life-threatening illness. Not everyone wants to receive care through a formal hospice program and others do not have hospice care programs available to them in their areas. Developing a support team may be one alternative open to such people.

The following ideas are not in any specific order. You might use some or all of the following ideas to develop a support team. Take only those ideas that apply to you and change or add ideas that meet the specific needs of the person who is ill. Remember that a support team is only effective when the person who has a terminal or life-threatening illness agrees with the idea and is an active participant in the decision making.

Keep in mind that the support team idea can be used in many different ways. In this book we look at how to help someone who has a terminal or life-threatening illness. It can just as easily be used for someone who has a chronic illness; for someone (old or young) who lives at home alone and needs some extra help to stay in their own home rather than move in with family or into an institution; for a parent who would like some time away from the children once or twice a week;

and for people who would like to increase their circle of friends. In other words, do not be limited by the ideas presented here. Let your imagination run wild with potential rather than with limitations.

Throughout the ideas presented here I will use the word friends to include family members and friends who do not live with the person who is ill, as well as volunteers who over time will probably become friends of the person.

1. It helps to have one or two friends act as the co-ordinator(s) of the support team. This person is generally not the spouse or closest loved one. The co-ordinator is responsible for organizing everyone's schedule for visiting the client (person who has a terminal or life-threatening illness). Freeing this responsibility from the closest loved one allows that loved one to concentrate on the person who is ill and vice versa rather than concentrating on the day-to-day details of scheduling and answering phone calls. It also gives the client and loved ones more time to relax, go out for walks, eat together quietly, and make plans for themselves and their family.

2. How do you recruit enough friends? How many do you need? Beth and Elaine suggested that a co-ordinator ask other friends for their help in visiting the client. As a co-ordinator (and not the client or immediate family) people would feel freer to say no if they did not want to participate. In this way there would be no hard feelings. People could be recruited from the family, friends and work colleagues who live in the area; people from clubs and organizations that the person belongs to (e.g. Rotary, volunteer work, veterans groups), and churches/synagogues/temples where the client worships. Another group that is often overlooked are neighbours. Neighbours are often willing to drop by with some food, help with running errands, cleaning up the outside (e.g. shovelling snow, mowing the lawn), or popping in early in the morning or late at night to help the person with getting up or going to bed.

3. The number of friends one person might need depends completely on the client and family's needs. Some people only want and need the help of a few close people. Other people may need more help, especially near the end of an illness. Trinity Hospice Toronto often schedules people into three-hour visits once every week or every two weeks if there are enough people. A general schedule they follow is:

9 p.m. - 8 a.m. (night visit if possible and necessary)
8 a.m. - 12 p.m.
12 p.m. - 3 p.m.
3 p.m. - 6 p.m.
6 p.m. - 9 p.m.

They find that if there are over-night visits the friend brings their own linen and often a change of clothes so that they can leave directly from the client's home to go to work or back to their own home ready to start the day.

If this schedule is followed it would require five people per day (other than the immediate family that lives with the client) or 35 people per week. Except for the night person, everyone commits to only a three-hour visit once a week. If you have 60-70 people, each person would only visit once every two weeks. Of course, some people would like to participate more often and that would be up to the client and family.

It is helpful for everyone on the team to have the monthly schedule and a list of all team members and their telephone numbers. Encourage team members to find their own replacements if they cannot make an appointment and let the co-ordinator know about any changes to the schedule.

4. As well as visiting the client at home, friends often meet once a month, or more often depending on the illness, to compare notes and feelings. Often clients participate in these meetings if they want or they may ask one of their family members to go. These meetings can be held in the client's home or elsewhere depending on the client's wishes and the space available.

5. What qualifications must a friend have? A friend is there to provide emotional support, practical help, companionship and to lessen the fear and isolation of the person who is ill and their family. Trinity Hospice states some of the qualifications as follows: motivated to help without interfering; emotional maturity; tolerance for different social cultural and religious beliefs; warmth, empathy, tact and discretion; flexibility; dependability; good listening skills; ability to work with others as a team member; different talents and skills (e.g. from past work experiences and hobbies); and a sense of humour (it is helpful not to take yourself too seriously). The key is to be there for the person and not to be there to fulfil your own, unspoken needs–to provide unconditional support and compassion.

5. Trinity Hospice Toronto recommends that clients use the services offered through the Home Care Program and homemaking services where available. These services will depend on the area you live in and may include: visits by nurses, physio/occupational therapists, social workers; homemaker help (e.g. to cook some meals, do dishes, do shopping and some light cleaning); and overnight nursing if available.

6. A log book is a helpful communication tool when more than a few people are involved in providing support at home. In this log book volunteers, professional caregivers (family doctor, visiting nurses) and family members can write notes about the likes and dislikes of the client, information that needs to be passed on to different people who will visit later that day or week, etc. The client often reads the comments and adds comments of her own. Some clients like the idea of a log book and others do not so check before hand. The book may also include information about what to do in an emergency, the person's provincial health care number, next of kin, medications, name and number of co- ordinator, and name and number of family physician. If for some reason the person needed to go to hospital the log book could be taken to provide up-to-date information.

7. Recognize that not everyone who wants to help the client will be appreciated, for various reasons. If the client prefers not to have someone come to their home, the co-ordinator would tell the person that the client's wishes are paramount and should not be taken personally. Some people do not "click" and that is perfectly acceptable. That person might still participate by cooking some meals, answering phones, etc. without having to see the client directly again.

8. Recognize that whenever a few people get together there will be tensions, misunderstandings and mistakes. People are doing their best but may do little things that annoy each other. Recognize these stresses and discuss them with others on a one- to-one basis or at general meetings if the problem goes beyond a few people. A example would be people who enter the client's home without taking off their shoes. This custom is perfectly acceptable in most people's homes but unacceptable in other people's homes. Knowing these little things will help make the experience more positive for everyone. The key is to remember that you are visiting someone's home where they are used to certain routines and behaviours. It is quite different from visiting that person in a hospital where their routines must blend in with the hospital's methods and expectations.

9. It is sometimes difficult to draw the line between providing support and making decisions for the client. We all have opinions and feelings about what a "dignified death" is. Some people believe that people should be at home, classical music playing in the background, afghan quilt on the bed, a dog or cat nearby, fresh flowers everywhere and the family and closest friends at the bedside. Other people prefer to go into hospital near the end of their lives to receive all the technological and emotional supports that round-the-clock hospital care can provide. Some people would like to be alone while others would like to have many people nearby. Regardless of your views and wishes, you must as a friend follow the wishes of the client as best you can. If you strongly disagree with a decision a client has made (on ethical or personal grounds) try to get another friend to be with the client. Call the co-ordinator to make different arrangements so that you do not have do to something against your strongly held beliefs and that the client does not have to give up control over their live in order to make you happy. This line between providing support and making decisions for a client should be discussed at most general meetings to help remind people of this gentle, yet vital, balance.

10. If the person is ill for a long time there will be friends who come and go because of other commitments. When new people come it is difficult at first for them to fit into what has probably become a tightly-knit group. For the client, who may be more ill than when the team began, it is one more person coming into their life and home. Recognize some of the difficulties and provide extra support to both the client and new person.

11. Friends will hear confidential information from the person who is ill and their family members. All this information is confidential and must not be repeated to anyone without permission. This includes telling one's own family and curious neighbours what is happening behind closed doors.

12. Use the talents you have rather than try to learn many new ones. Find people who have the skills and interests you miss so that you can concentrate on giving that part of yourself to someone else that you are both most comfortable with. For example, you may enjoy reading and writing and could help the person with their mail or reading a book with them. Someone else may help without necessarily being with the person who is ill. They may enjoy cooking, cleaning, gardening, walking the dog, or running errands without having to spend time with the person. Other people may enjoy helping the person eat their food, doing arts and crafts together, or doing bookkeeping, financial or legal matters together (or alone). "Being there" is also a wonderful gift. Sometimes people don't want to talk, listen or do things. They want to rest, think, pray or day dream. Being there means that you do not interrupt but give them the privacy or companionship the person wants.

13. If you are interested in this kind of friendship you may want to read some of the books or articles in the field of palliative care (see Recommended Readings section), attend some volunteer training workshops and talk to other people about these possibilities. Active participation is the best teacher but other ways of learning can also help you.

14. People who have a cold, flu or infection should not visit the client until they feel better themselves. You would not want to pass on the illness to the person.

Spending time with someone who has a terminal or life-threatening illness is very rewarding and can also be very traumatic. Friends must take care of themselves and each other as much as they try to help the client. People need to talk about their experiences. People need time to think about what they are experiencing. Take the time and make the efforts. Having helped my parents and my grandfather live at home until their death are some of my richest experiences. I learned so much about them and so much about myself. I took the time to try to understand what I was thinking and feeling. There were many happy moments and many sad ones. The wealth of that experience will sustain me for the rest of my life. Enjoy the learning. Enjoy the giving. Enjoy the receiving.

For further information on palliative care support teams write or call Trinity Hospice Toronto: 10 Trinity Square, Toronto, Ontario, M5G 1B1, Canada – (416) 599-0736.

If you are interested in the idea of offering support to people who may, or may not, have a terminal or life-threatening illness you might also check your phone book to see if you have a local Citizen Advocacy organization in your area. According to Cecile Lynes, Co-ordinator of Toronto Citizen Advocacy, "citizen advocates are ordinary community people who are recruited specifically for a person we know who is isolated, marginalized and vulnerable for any number of reasons. Citizen advocates learn by listening to the stories of their vulnerable friends, by walking in their shoes, by experiencing for a time what life is like where their friends live or work or spend time. "

"Sometimes, in Citizen Advocacy, an advocate will bring a group of people together [similar to Trinity Hospice Toronto's support teams but not limited to people who are dying] around an individual who has a disability, and together they will decide what needs to be done. Some groups or 'circles' as they are sometimes called, are very focused around a specific goal such as getting a person out of an institution or working to include a child in his or her neighbourhood school in a regular classroom, or helping a person to find a job. "

"People within the group may have different responsibilities which they undertake at particular times. The idea of 'circles' extends beyond people with disabilities. It may have evolved from simpler times when a neighbour could be counted on to look after your children when you needed a break or got sick, or when you talked to friends about a possible career change. Some people are still able to draw on personal, informal supports. Others may choose to use a professional service for such support, while others may be forced through lack of options into the service world. If people can draw on their own natural supports, they may be able to stay out of the service world and thus maintain control over their lives."

For more information about Citizen Advocacy you may contact Toronto Citizen Advocacy, 455 Spadina Avenue, Suite 306, Toronto, Ontario, M5S 2G8, (416) 597-1131.

RECOMMENDED READINGS

The following is an updated selection of recommended readings and books. They certainly do not include all the books available on the various subjects in this book. My first recommendation is that you check your local book store and library for the most recent and up-to-date books on the topic you are most interested in. This updated list of references includes books published after the first printing of Choices. The annotated list of books published after 1985 was compiled by Mary Hazel of the Anglican Book Centre, 600 Jarvis Street, Toronto, Ontario, M4Y 2J6; (416) 924-9192. This centre has the most complete selection of books in the field of dying and death that I have found. I appreciate Mary's help in providing this abbreviated annotated list of some of the many books available through the Centre.

There are books that fit into more than one category, so please look in several categories for the books that will help you.

GENERAL INTEREST BOOKS

Although these books are recommended for the general public they would also be useful for caregivers involved in the care and treatment of people with terminal illness and their families. As well books listed in the section recommended for professional caregivers may also be of interest to the general public.

Berry, Carmen Rene. **When Helping You is Hurting Me: Escaping the Messiah Trap.** New York: Harper and Row, 1989. *Provides fresh insights into the problems of neglecting one's personal needs in order to help others.*

Brody, Jane E. **Jane Brody's The New York Times Guide to Personal Health.** New York: Avon, 1982. 724 pp. *An example of an encyclopedic health education text. Every home should have some kind of health encyclopedia.*

Buckman, Robert. **I Don't Know What to Say: How to Help and Support Someone Who is Dying.** Toronto: Key Porter, 1989. *A book written specifically for the friends and family of a dying person.*

Cameron, Jean. **For All That Has Been: Time to Live and Time to Die.** New York: Macmillan Publishing Company, Inc., 1982. *Book by a hospital social worker with terminal cancer who describes her work on a palliative care unit, her struggle with cancer that keeps growing and bereavement concerns. She lives the Viktor Frankl observation that our last human freedom is our ability to choose our response to whatever the circumstances.*

Carroll, David. **Living With Dying: A Loving Guide for Family and Close Friends.** New York: McGraw-Hill Book Company, 1985. 381 pp. *Question and answer format covering the emotional and physical needs of the patient, family and friends.*

Cousins, Norman. **Anatomy of an Illness As Perceived by the Patient.** Toronto: Bantam Books, 1979. *How this magazine editor overcame a terminal illness using common sense, laughter, learning about his condition and taking personal control over his health. Also interviews Pablo Cassals and Albert Schweitzer.*

Hanson, Peter G., M.D. **The Joy of Stress.** Toronto: Hanson Stress Management Organization, 1985. 223 pp. *Examines physical and mental causes and effects of stress and how to turn stress into a positive, energizing force.*

Inlander, Charles B. with Ed Weiner. **Take This Book to the Hospital With You.** Emmaus, Pennsylvania: Rodale Press, 1985. 223 pp. *People's Medical Society consumer guide for patients going into hospital.*

Kavanaugh, Robert E. **Facing Death.** Los Angeles: Nash, 1972. *Sensitive account of a personal and professional approach to facing death and meeting the emotional needs of someone who is dying.*

Kubler-Ross, Elisabeth. **Questions and Answers on Death and Dying.** New York: Macmillan Publishing Co. Inc., 1974. 177 pp. *Question-and-answer format concerning dying, communication, care, psychological effects, funerals, staff stress and old age.*

Lamm, Maurice. **The Jewish Way in Death and Mourning.** New York: Jonathan David Publishers, 1969. 265 pp. *The Jewish traditions re: preparation of the body after death for the funeral and burial, the funeral service, the mourning observances including year-long observances, special situations and life after death.*

Levine, Stephen. **Who Dies? An Investigation of Conscious Living and Conscious Dying.** New York: Anchor Press, 1982. *Examines evidence of reincarnation.*

Moody, Raymond A., Jr. **Life After Life: the Investigation of a Phenomenon, Survival of Bodily Death.** Harrisburg, P.A.: Stackpole Books, 1976. 125 pp. *Based on interviews with people who were "dead" but revived, Moody examines 15 points that bind all these peoples' experiences together.*

-----. **Reflections on Life After Life.** Harrisburg, P.A.: Stackpole Books, 1977. 140 pp. *Further interviews and conclusions on life-after-death issues.*

Morgan, Ernest. **A Manual of Death Education and Simple Burial, 19th Edition.** Burnsville, NC: Celo Press, 1984. 156 pp. *Review of death education, home care, bereavement, right-to-die issues, simple burials and a bibliography.*

St. John Ambulance. **The Complete Handbook of Family Health Care.** Ottawa: St. John Priory of Canada, 1984. *Review of home care, medication, bed care, cleaning and treatments.*

GENERAL INTEREST BOOKS FOR PROFESSIONAL CAREGIVERS

The resources listed below are more technical in nature and often written specifically for professional caregivers but may also be interesting for non-professionals.

Adler, Robert (ed). **Psychoneuroimmunology.** New York: Academic Press,

1981. 661 pp. *Comprehensive study of the role of emotions and stress to the immune system and its effects on infection resistance, allergies and cancer.*

Backer, Barbara A., Natalie Hannon and Noreen A. Russell. **Death and Dying: Individuals and Institutions.** New York: John Wiley & Sons, 1982. 332 pp. *Emphasizes caring versus curing aspects of health care with interdisciplinary approach using exercises, A.V. materials and references for nurses, social workers, and sociology, psychology and medical students.*

Bowers, Margaretta K., Edgar Jackson, James Knight & Lawrence LeShan. **Counselling the Dying.** New York: Harper and Row, 1981. 180 pp. *Series of short essays on counselling including religious, psychotherapy, philosophical and moral implications of couselling.*

Charles-Edwards, A. **The Nursing Care of the Dying Patient.** New York: Beaconsfield Publishers, 1983. *Comprehensive guide to the spiritual, psychological and practical aspects of helping someone who is dying including specific nursing care and pain relief.*

Chidwick, Paul. **Dying Yet We Live.** Toronto: Anglican Book Centre, 1988. *Our response to the spiritual needs of people who are dying.*

Columbia University Press. **Foundation of Thanatology Series.** *Includes such topics as psychological aspects of terminal care, anticipatory grief, bereavement, nurse as caregiver and others.*

Copperman, H. **Dying at Home.** Chichester: John Wiley, 1983. *For those caring for someone at home including emotional support to patient and family, symptom control, care in the final days and the needs of the bereaved.*

Fairchild, Ray W. **Finding Hope Again: A Pastor's Guide to Counselling the Depressed.** New York: Harper and Row, 1980. 150 pp. *Review of pastoral counselling examining such issues as the different types of depression, the meaning of hope, working with health professionals, various strategies and work with the bereaved.*

Feifel, Herman (ed.). **New Meanings of Death.** New York: McGraw-Hill, 1977. *Updated version of his earlier collection of academic essays.*

Gentles, Ian (ed). **Care for the Dying and the Bereaved.** Toronto: Anglican Book Centre, 1982. 160 pp. *Various issues of palliative care and dying at home plus bereavement, children with terminal illness, anti-euthanasia and Christian dying.*

Grollman, Earl Alan (ed). **Concerning Death: A Practical Guide for the Living.** Boston: Beacon Press, 1974. 365 pp. *Question-and-answer format dealing with most aspects of dying including grief, care, physicians, children, religions, funerals, organ donations and emotional help from friends. Each section has an extensive bibliography.*

Omega International Journal for the Psychological Study of Dying, Bereavement, Suicide and other Lethal Behaviours. Westport, Connecticut: Greenwood Press, Inc. 51 Riverside Avenue, 06880.

Pattison, E. Mansell (ed). **The Experience of Dying.** Englewood Cliffs, N.J.:

Prentice-Hall Inc., 1977. 336 pp. *Clinical approach for caregivers of people dying in early childhood, middle childhood, adolescence, middle age and the elderly.*

Platt, Nancy Van Dyke. **Pastoral Care to the Cancer Patient.** Springfield, IL: Charles C. Thomas, 1980. *Spiritual care for patients with a terminal illness.*

Simonton, O. Carl, M.D., Stephanie Matthews-Simonton, James Creighton. **Getting Well Again.** Los Angeles: J. P. Tarcher, Inc., 1978. 268 pp. *Examines connections between the mind and cancer and how relaxation, mental imaging and improved diet and exercise can help people with cancer.*

Stillion, Judith M. **Death and the Sexes: An Examination of the Differential Longevity, Attitudes, Behaviours and Coping Skills.** New York: Hemisphere Publishing Corporation, 1985. 166 pp. *Sexism in death, sex differences in longevity, sex roles and death attitudes, bereavement and grief, death education & counselling.*

Turnbull, Richard (ed). **Terminal Care.** Washington, DC: Hemisphere Publishing Corp., 1986. 282 pp. *Symptom control, bereavement, staff stress and education plus terminal care in rural areas.*

Turner, Gerald P. and Joseph Mapa (eds). **Humanizing Hospital Care.** New York: McGraw-Hill Ryerson, 1979. 233 pp. *Academic articles on humanizing medicine, erosion of professional authority, good and problem patients, awareness of cultural differences, indignity of illness, patient as consumer, hospice care, holistic health.*

Wass, Hannelore and Charles A. Corr (eds). **Childhood and Death.** Washington, DC: Hemisphere Publishing Corp., 1984. 392 pp. *Resource for caregivers dealing with death and children including recommended books for children and adults and A.V. resources.*

-----. **Helping Children Cope with Death Guidelines and Resources, 2nd edition.** Washington, DC: Hemisphere Publishing Corp., 1984. *Part of a series of books looking at childrens' thoughts about death, death education and recommended books for adults and children of all ages.*

Wass, Hannelore, C.A. Corr, R.A. Pacholski and C.M. Forfar. **Death Education: An Annotated Resource Guide, II.** Washington, DC: Hemisphere Publishing Corp., 1985. *Primarily for teachers in death education but also for other caregivers, with an extensive lists of books, articles, texts, bibliographies, A.V. resources, organizational resources, community resources. Part of a series of guides in Death Education.*

Weisman, Avery D., M.D. **On Dying and Denying: A Psychiatric Study of Terminality.** New York: Behavioural Publishing, 1972. 247 pp. *Describes psychological stages a person with a terminal illness may go through plus description of first, second and third order denial.*

PALLIATIVE/HOSPICE CARE

Ajemian, Ina and Balfour M. Mount. **The R.V.H. Manual on Palliative/Hospice Care.** New York: Arno Press, 1980. 556 pp. *Extensive manual an all facits of palliative care.*

Corr, Charles A. Ph.D., and Donna M. Corr, R.N., B.S.N. (eds). **Hospice Care: Principles and Practice.** New York: Springer Publishing Company, 1983. 364 pp. *Resource for professionals dealing in any aspect of palliative care including pain control techniques, nursing care, hospice organization, volunteers, and death education.*

Hall, Beverly. **Caring for the Dying: A Guide for Caregivers in Home and Hospital.** Toronto: Anglican Book Centre, 1988. *A practical guide for both professionals and volunteers.*

Krieger, Dolores, Ph.D., R.N. **The Therapeutic Touch.** Englewood Cliffs, N.J.: Prentice-Hall, Inc., 1979. 168 pp. *A how-to book describing the therapeutic touch technique of natural healing taught in various universities in the U.S.*

Kutscher, Austin H. and Samuel C. Klagsbrum et. al. (eds) **Hospice U.S.A..** New York: Columbia University Press, 1983. 300 pp. *A review of the hospice movement in the U.S. including ethical and human issues of terminal care, approach to helping the dying and alternatives to in-hospice care.*

Munley, Anne. **The Hospice Alternative: A New Concept for Death and Dying.** New York: Basic Books, Inc., 1983. 349 pp. *A professionals' guide and education into hospice care.*

Munro, Susan. **Music Therapy in Palliative/Hospice Care.** New York: Gustav Fischer Verlag Stuttgart, 1984. 112 pp. *For professionals and volunteers; includes case studies and guidelines.*

Saunders, Cicely. **Hospice and Palliative Care.** London: Edward Arnold, 1990. *Written jointly by a team of experts in the field, this book offers good advice for setting up an interdisciplinary team on caring for the dying.*

Saunders, Cicely. **Hospice: The Living Idea.** London: Edward Arnold, 1991. *To help the health care professional understand how hospice care focuses on the quality of life left to the patient.*

Spilling, R. **Terminal Care at Home.** Oxford University Press, 1986. *This book is intended to improve the comfort of those choosing to die at home, and to increase the proportion of those able to do so.*

Taylor, Joan Leslie. **In the Light of Dying: The Journals of a Hospice Volunteer.** New York: Continuum, 1989. *A sensitive account of the loving relationships between hospice volunteers, patients and caregivers.*

van Bommel, Harry. **Dying for Care: Hospice Care and Euthanasia.** Toronto: NC Press. 1992. *An examination of the need for more hospice care programs (informal and formal) before society spends much time, effort and resources on the euthanasia debate. Includes detailed quotes from Canadian hospice care leaders.*

PAIN AND SYMPTOM CONTROL

Many of the books listed in the section for professionals have specific chapters on pain and symptom control. The following deal more specifically with pain and symptom control plus a list of pharmaceutical texts:

Angel, Jack E. (Publisher). **Physicians' Desk Reference 38th Edition.** Oradell, N.J.: Medical Economics Company Inc., 1984. 3040 pp. plus supplements. *Standard physicians' text on all prescription drugs, their purpose and their side effects.*

Autton, Norman. **Pain—An Exploration.** London: Darton, Longman & Todd, 1989. *The fruit of an enormous amount of work, experience and reading.*

Canadian Pharmaceutical Association. **About Your Medicines.** Ottawa, 1982. *Consumer's guide to drugs.*

-----. **Compendium of Pharmaceuticals and Specialties.** Ottawa. *Choose most recent edition for professional information on drugs.*

Expert Advisory Committee on the Management of Severe Chronic Pain in Cancer Patients. **Cancer Pain: A Monograph on the Management of Cancer Pain.** Ottawa: Ministry of Supply and Services, 1984. 40 pp. *Excellent summary of modern pain control techniques and distributed to all Canadian physicians.*

Goldberg, Ivan K., Austin H. Kutscher and Sidney Malitz (eds). **Pain, Anxiety & Grief: Pharmacotherapeutic Care of the Dying Patient and the Bereaved.** New York: Columbia University Press, 1986. 232 pp. *Series of professional articles.*

Saunders, Cicely M. (ed). **The Management of Terminal Disease.** London: Edward Arnold (Publishers), 2nd Ed., 1984. *Gives specific drugs and doses for pain control plus other forms of symptom control including radiation, chemotherapy, surgery and philosophy of palliative care.*

Smoller, Bruce, M.D. and Brian Schulman, M.D. **Pain Control: The Bethesday Program.** New York: Doubleday and Company, Inc., 1982. *Defines pain, pain zones, coping with chronic pain and effects on the family plus use of exercise, diet, relaxation, pain diary and sex.*

Saunders, Cicely and Baines, Mary. **Living with Dying: The Management of Terminal Disease.** Oxford University Press, 1989. *A clinical examination of terminal illness.*

Twycross, Robert and Lack, Sylvia A. **Therapeutics in Terminal Care.** New York: Churchill Livingstone, 1990. *A highly practical, quick reference book for all those involved in the care of cancer patients.*

CHRONIC ILLNESS

Adams, Martha O. **Alzheimer's Disease: A Call to Courage for Caregivers.** Saint Meinrad, IN: Abbey Press, 1987. *Written from personal experience the author emphasizes the practical care of the Alzheimer's patient.*

Cleveland, Martha. **Living Well: A twelve-step response to chronic illness and disability.** New York: Harper-Collins, 1989. *Wisdom for millions who suffer from the distress and pain of chronic illness and disability.*

Lester, Bonnie. **Women & AIDS.** New York: Continuum, 1989. *A helpful book written for women caregivers who must first confront their own feelings about AIDS before they can help others.*

Mace, Nancy and Rabins, Peter. **The 36-Hour Day: A Family Guide to Caring for Persons with Alzheimer's Disease, Related Dementing Illness and Memory Loss in Later Life.** Baltimore, MD: John Hopkins, 1991. *A family guide to caring for persons with Alzheimer's Disease, related dementing illness and memory loss in later life.*

Maurer, Janet. R. and Strasberg, Patricia D. **Building a New Dream: A Family Guide to Coping with Chronic Illness and Disability.** Redding, MA: Addison Wesley, 1990. *A guide for patients, family and friends of anyone facing chronic illness. It provides practical and wise advice on coping with a changed life.*

Miller, Judith F. **Coping with Chronic Illness: Overcoming Powerlessness.** New York: Davis, 1983. *A book offered as a resource for caregivers and patients to help combat the sense of helplessness in chronic illness.*

Moffat, Betty Clare. **When Someone You Love Has AIDS.** New York: Plume. *One family's courage and togetherness in the midst of catastrophe.*

Schwartzentruber, Michael. **From Crisis to New Creation.** Winfield, BC: Wood Lake, 1988. *A terminally ill young man suffering from cystic fibrosis probes "all that I would like to be", with hope, sensitivity and courage.*

Starkie, John and Dale, Rodney. **Understanding AIDS.** New York: Hodder & Stoughton, 1989. *A factual guide that confronts the fears and prejudices of AIDS, plus practical advice.*

LEGAL AND MORAL RIGHTS AND RESPONSIBILITIES

Annas, George J. **The Rights of Hospital Patients.** New York: Avon Books, 1975. 246 pp. *By the American Civil Liberties Union this question-and-answer format book examines all areas of a patient's hospital rights.*

-----, Leonard H. Glantz, Barbara F. Katz. **The Rights of Doctors, Nurses, and Allied Health Professionals.** Cambridge, Mass.: Ballinger Publishing Company, 1981. 382 pp. *American Civil Liberties Union's examination of caregivers' rights to practice, the caregiver-patient relationship and liability and income rights.*

The Hastings Centre. **Guidelines on the Termination of Life-Sustaining Treatment and the Care of the Dying.** Bloomington: Indiana University, 1988. *A record of cases which highlight medical, ethical, legal, psychological dilemmas.*

Robertson, John A. **The Rights of the Critically Ill.** New York: Bantam Books, 1983. 171 pp. *American Civil Liberties Union book in a question-and-answer format.*

Rozovsky, Lorne Elkin. **The Canadian Patient's Book of Rights.** Toronto: Doubleday Canada Limited, 1980. 162 pp. *Patient rights in Canada with a list of provincial licensing authorities, medical associations, and nursing associations.*

Storch, J. **Patients' Rights: Ethical and Legal Issues in Health Care and Nursing.** Toronto: McGraw-Hill Ryerson Limited, 1982. 249 pp. *For health care professionals, this book reviews patients' rights, the ethics and law plus an extensive bibliography.*

EUTHANASIA ISSUES

Barnard, Christiaan, M.D. **Good Life Good Death: A Doctor's Case for Euthanasia and Suicide.** Englewood Cliffs, N.J.: Prentice-Hall, Inc. 1980. 146 pp.

Heifetz, Milton D., M.D. with Charles Mangel. **The Right to Die.** New York: G. P. Putnam and Sons, 1975. 246 pp. *Neurosurgeon, who consulted on the Karen Quinlan case, presents his argument for the right to die with dignity.*

Humphry, Derek. **Final Exit: The Practicalities of Self-Deliverance and Assisted Suicide for the Dying.** Eugene, OR: Hemlock Society, 1991. *A book with specific information on assisted suicides for people with a terminal illness.*

Humphry, Derek and Ann Wickett. **The Right to Die.** New York: Harper and Row, Publishers, 1986. *Complete historical review of euthanasia plus and examination of the modern moral and legal issues.*

Law Reform Commission of Canada. **Report on Euthanasia, Aiding Suicide and Cessation of Treatment.** Ottawa: Ministry of Supply and Services Canada, 1983. *An overview of the legal and moral issues regarding euthanasia and final recommendations regarding the Canadian Criminal Code.*

Maguire, Daniel C. **Death By Choice, 2nd Edition.** New York: Image Books/Doubleday and Co. Inc., 1984. 224 pp. *A Catholic theologian's examination of the ethics of various forms of euthanasia, abortion and suicide including his argument for euthanasia under certain circumstances.*

The Position of the Royal Dutch Medical Association on Euthanasia English translation by e.t.c. (English Text Company), Nassau Dillenburgstraat 16, 2596 AD, Den Haag, August 1984. *Criteria by which Dutch physicians are permited to commit active euthanasia.*

Report of the Dutch Government's Commission on Euthanasia 19 August 1985. *English summary of this report is provided by the Nederlandse Verineging voor Vrijwillege Euthanasie. Examines legal issues and possible legislative changes to permit euthanasia.*

van Bommel, Harry. **Dying for Care: Hospice Care and Euthanasia.** Toronto: NC Press. 1992. *An examination of the need for more hospice care programs (informal and formal) before much time, effort and resources are dedicated to the euthanasia debate. Includes quotes from Canadian hospice care leaders.*

BEREAVEMENT AND GRIEVING

Many of the books listed in the general interest sections have specific chapters dealing with bereavement for adults and children plus the anticipatory grieving of patients. The following books deal more specifically with these concerns.

Bernstein, Joanne and Gullo, Stephen. **When People Die.** New York: Dutton, 1977. *For Grades 1-6 this book explains theories of afterlife, grief, burial practices and how death is a natural part of the chain of life.*

Bluebond-Langner, M. **The Private Worlds of Dying Children.** New York:

Princeton University Press, 1978. *An analysis of dying children's behaviour based on observation and author's personal involvement with children, parents and caregivers.*

Buckman, Robert. **Care of the Dying Child: A Practical Guide for Those Who Help Others.** New York: Continuum, 1988. *A comprehensive book dealing with various concerns related to the care of the terminally ill child and family.*

Campbell, Scott and Silverman, Phyllis. **Widower.** New York: Prentice Hall, 1987. *True stories of men left alone and how they coped.*

Coburn, John. **Anne and the Sand Dobbies.** Ridgefield, CT: Morehouse/Barlow, 1986. *A story to help parents and children face the unavoidable fact of death squarely.*

Fassier, Joan. **My Grandpa Died Today.** New York: Human Sciences Press, 1971. *Picture book for children of all ages tells how a young boy adjusts to his grandfather's death.*

Foehner, Charlotte and Cozart, Carol. **The Widow's Handbook: A Guide for Living.** Golden, CO: Fulcrum, 1987. *An extremely practical book full of sound basic information for a newly widowed individual.*

Furman, Erma. **A Child's Parent Dies.** New Haven, Conn.: Yale University Press, 1974. *Case studies by psychiatrists of children whose parent has died.*

Gordon, Audrey and Klass, Dennis. **They Need to Know, How to Teach Children About Death.** Englewood Cliffs, N.J.: Prentice-Hall, 1979. *Resource for parents, social workers and educators.*

Grollman, Earl Alan (ed). **Explaining Death to Children.** Boston: Beacon Press, 1976. *Chapters by professionals and clergy. All of Grollman's books are filled with practical information.*

-----. **Living When A Loved One Has Died.** Boston: Beacon Press, 1977.

-----. **Talking about Death: A Dialogue Between Parent and Child.** Boston: Beacon Press, 1991. *An excellent book to use with grieving children. The winner of the UNESCO Book Award.*

-----. **When Your Loved One is Dying.** Boston: Beacon Press, 1980.

Krementz, Jill. **How It Feels When a Parent Dies.** New York: Knoph, 1988. *Eighteen children speak openly and honestly of their feelings when a parent dies.*

Kubler-Ross, Elisabeth. **On Children and Death.** New York: Macmillan Publishing Company, 1983. 279 pp. *Includes an extensive bibliography.*

Kushner, Harold S. **When Bad Things Happen to Good People.** New York: Avon Books, 1981. *A distinguished clergyman's explanation of how God does not cause bad things but rather provides strength and courage to cope with difficult situations.*

LeShan, Eda. **Learning to Say Good-by: When A Parent Dies.** New York: Avon Books, 1976. 124 pp. *A non-fiction book for Grade 5 through High School on death, grief, recovering from grief and what death teaches us about life.*

Parkes, Colin Murray, M.D. **Bereavement: Studies of Grief in Adult Life.** London: Tavistockand Pelican, 1972. *A classic work in studying grief.*

Rando, Therese A. **Grief, Dying and Death.** Champaign, IL: Research Press, 1984. *A clinically oriented examination of grief and loss for the professional caregiver, focusing on practical applications for caregiving.*

Rando, Therese A. **Loss and Anticipatory Grief.** New York: Free Press, 1986. *This book will help all who work with the dying bereaved to understand the many forms of anticipatory grief and use the forwarning of loss in a positive and creative way.*

Rando, Therese, A. **Parental Loss of a Child.** New York: Research Press, 1986. *An in-depth study of the unique needs of parents suffering from the loss of a child.*

Romond, Janis Loomis. **Children Facing Grief: Letters from bereaved brothers and sisters.** Saint Meinrad, IN: Abbey Press, 1989. *A book for bereaved families, a tool to open communications between children and parents.*

Rosen, Helen. **Unspoken Grief.** New York: Free Press, 1986. *A study of the effect of sibling death on a child and their family.*

Sandford, Doris. **It Must Hurt a Lot.** Portland, OR: Multnomah Press, 1985. *For children between the ages of 5 and 11. A touching story about a boy whose puppy is killed by a car.*

Schneiderman, Gerald. **Coping with Death in the Family.** Toronto: NC Press, 1985. 168 pp. *Reviews death of an infant, child, adolescence, a parent's death, a grandparent's death, widow/ers and your own death.*

Viorst, Judith. **The Tenth Good Thing About Barney.** New York: Atheneum Publications, 1975. *For Grades K-4 this picture book tells about the death and burial of some childrens' cat.*

Watts, Richard G. **Strangest Talk About Death with Young People.** Philadelphia: Westminster Press, 1975. *Question-and-answer format for Grade 7 and 8 students looking at facts about death, what it is like to die, understanding grief and funerals and hopes people live by and die by.*

Worden, William J. **Grief Counselling and Grief Therapy.** New York: Springer Publishing Company, Inc., 1982. *A professional reference for counsellors and therapists and often used as a starting reference for professionals.*

PERSONAL STORIES

Brady, Mari. **Please Remember Me: A Young Woman's Story of Her Friendship with an Unforgettable 15 Year Old Boy.** New York: Doubleday and Company Inc., 1977. 104 pp. *Brady was a recreational aid and worked with young cancer patients.*

Brown, Tom. **Jeannette: A Memoir.** Toronto: Lester and Orpen Limited, 1978. 217 pp. *Nine day story of his wife's death and his examination why he couldn't help her with euthanasia as she had asked.*

Caine, Lynn. **Widow.** New York: Bantam Books, 1975. *Her examination of how she grieved her husband's loss, her anger at his death and how she coped.*

Callwood, June. **Jim: A Life with AIDS.** Toronto: Lester & Orpen Dennys. 1990. *Jim's story will inform and enlighten everyone who seeks a better understanding of the ever increasing tragedy of AIDS.*

Callwood, June. **Twelve Weeks of Spring.** Toronto: Lester & Orpen Dennys, 1986. *The story of Margaret Frazer's life ending in vitality and love, a triumphant experiment in palliative care.*

Craven, Margaret. **I Heard the Owl Call My Name.** Toronto: A Totem Book, 1975. 133 pp. *Story of a young Anglican priest sent to an British Columbian Indian Village. He doesn't know he is terminally ill yet learns "enough of life to be ready to die."*

Kennedy, Betty. **Gerhard: A Love Story.** Toronto: Macmillan of Canada Limited, 1976. 95 pp. *A journalist/broadcaster's sensitive story of her husband's last year and how they dealt with his dying.*

Rollin, Betty. **Last Wish.** New York: Signet, 1985. *How her mother asked to die with dignity before her ovarian cancer incapacitated her and how Rollin did the research to discover what drugs would best help her die peacefully.*

Sarton, May. **A Reckoning.** New York: W.W. Norton and Company, 1981. *A fictional account of a dying woman's examination of her life and relationships with family and friends.*

Weinman-Lear, Martha. **Heartsounds.** New York: Pocket Books, 1980. 501 pp. *A journalist's story of her urologist husband's loosing battle with degenerative heart disease. It describes a surgeon's frustration and anger at being treated like a child by the medical profession and how he recognizes how he might have done the same with his patients. His wife describes what it is like to help a spouse die.*

GLOSSARY

The following list includes medical and legal definitions, descriptions of various medical specialists, and common abbreviations used on medical charts and prescriptions. For a complete definition use a more extensive standard medical or legal dictionary.

a.c. abbrev. = before meals.

Acupressure A method of pain relief using finger pressure on the same points used in acupuncture.

Acupuncture Chinese medical practice of using needles inserted through the skin in specific points to restore the balance of a body's energy flow.

Acute Condition with symptoms that develop quickly, are severe, but do not last long. Opposite to chronic condition.

Addiction Uncontrollable craving for a substance with an increasing tolerance and physical dependence on it.

Allergist Often an Internist who also specializes in the treatments of allergies.

Allergy A reaction to environmental factors or substances which may cause a rash, swelling or more serious physical response.

Amyotrophic Lateral Sclerosis (ALS) A deterioration of the spinal cord resulting in the wasting away of muscles.

Analgesic A pain-relieving drug.

Anaphylaxis An exaggerated, often serious, allergic reaction to proteins and other substances.

Anemia A deficiency in red blood corpuscles or in hemoglobin content of the red corpuscles.

Anesthesia Total or partial loss of sensation from an injection, ingestion or inhalation of a drug.

Anesthesiologist A physician specializing in providing an anesthetic during surgery and monitoring patient's vital signs.

Aneurysm A swollen or distended area in a blood vessel wall.

Angiogram X-ray studies in which a dye is injected into the bloodstream to detect abnormalities in blood vessels, tissues and organs.

Antacid A substance that neutralizes acid.

Antibiotic Drugs that check the growth of bacteria but do not work against viruses.

Antibody A substance produced in our bodies to fight against disease organisms.

Assets All of a person's properties, including real estate, cash, stocks and bonds, art, furniture etc., and claims against other people (e.g. loans).

Atrophy A wasting or withering away of part of a body.

Autopsy An examination of a dead body to determine the cause of death; the post-mortem ordered by coroner or medical examiner.

Barbituate A type of sleeping pill.

Barium Enema Radiopaque barium (visible by x-ray) is put into the lower bowel (colon) and rectum by an enema for an x-ray. Also called a Lower GI Series.

Bed Sore Sore caused by pressure-induced skin ulceration as a result of inadequate blood circulation to the skin. For persons confined to bed, good skin care, repositioning, cushioning and some limited activity are the best treatment.

Beneficiary Person who receives a benefit from a will, insurance policy or trust fund.

Benign Non-malignant self-limiting condition that is not life-threatening.

b.i.d. abbrev. = twice a day.

Biopsy The microscopic examination of a portion of body tissue to help in diagnosis. Tissue removed from body by surgery, insertion of needle into tissue and other methods.

Blood Gas Test A blood test to determine the level of oxygen and carbon dioxide in the blood.

Bone Marrow Test A needle is inserted into a bone (hipbone or breatbone) to remove a sample of bone marrow for diagnostic purposes e.g. to diagnose leukemia, aplastic anemia.

Brain Scan More properly called carotid angiogram. A radioactive substance is injected into a neck artery for a brain x-ray using a scanning camera.

CAT Scan A Computerized Axial Tomography scan. A body or head, computer-driven x-ray that gives slice-by-slice view of region.

CCU Coronary Care Unit in a hospitial which provides intensive care of heart patients.

Cancer A malignant tumor that tends to invade healthy tissue and spread to new sites.

Cardiac Surgeon Physicians specializing in heart surgery.

Cardiologist Physician specializing in diagnosis and treatment of heart conditions.

Cardiovascular Surgeon Physician specializing in surgery of blood vessels associated with the heart.

c.c. abbrev. = cubic centimetre.

Cerebral Palsy Impaired muscular power and coordination from failure of nerve cells in the brain.

Chemotherapy Drug therapy against infection or malignancy designed to destroy bacteria or offending cells.

Chiropractor Non-physicians specializing in manipulation of the spine; cannot prescribe medication or perform surgery.

Chronic A prolonged or lingering condition.

Codicil An appendix or supplement to a will (e.g. to change the name of your beneficiary).

COPD Chronic Obstructive Pulmonary (Lung) Disease. Includes such illnesses as emphysema.

Colostomy A surgical opening from the body surface (usually through the abdomen) into the colon which acts as an artificial anus. Colostomy bags collect the body's waste. Depending on a patient's condition a colostomy may be temporary.

Coma A deep, prolonged unconsciousness.

Congenital Something present since birth.

Cystoscopy A long flexible tube, attached to a miniature camera, is passed through the urinary tract into the bladder to get a direct view for diagnosis and possible treatment. Avoids need for exploratory surgery.

d. abbrev. = give.

dd. in d abbrev. = from day to day.

dec abbrev. = pour off.

Dementia Deterioration of a person's mental capacity from changes in the brain.

Depressant A drug to reduce mental or physical activity.

Dermatologist Physician specializing in skin conditions.

Diagnosis An analysis of someone's physical and/or mental condition.

dil abbrev. = dilute.

Disp. abbrev. = dispense.

Diuretic A drug to increase urine output, relieving edema.

Doctor Common title for a physician. Technically a doctor holds the highest academic degree awarded by a university in fields as different as Doctor of Music, Doctor of Divinity or Doctor of English.

dos abbrev. = dose.

dur dolor abbrev. = while pain lasts.

Dx abbrev. = diagnosis.

ECG See EKG.

EKG (Electrocardiogram) A record of the minute electrical currents produced by the heart. Of value in diagnosing abnormal cardiac rhythm and myocardial damage. Also ECG.

EEG (Electroencephalogram) A record of the minute electrical currents produced by the brain.

Edema Excess collection of fluid in the tissues.

Embolism Blockage of a blood artery by a clot. In the brain it can cause a stroke.

EMG (Electromyography) Test to evaluate the electrical activity of nerves and muscles.

emp abbrev. = as directed.

Emphysema A condition of the lungs marked by labored breathing and increased susceptibility to infection. Includes the loss of elasticity and function of lungs.

Endocrinologist A specialist in diagnosing and treating disorders of the endocrine glands (glands affecting hormones) and their secretions.

Enema A fluid injected into the rectum to clean out the bowel or to administer drugs.

Estate All of one's assets and liabilities, especially those left by a deceased.

Executor The person named in a will to dispose of the assets and pay, from estate funds, the liabilities of a deceased.

Executrix The female noun for executor.

Family Practitioner Physician who diagnoses and treats the general illnesses and problems of patients and refers them to a specialist when necessary.

febris Latin for fever.

FRCP[C] abbreviated title for Fellow of the Royal College of Physicians. [C] represents Canadian College. Requires a further 4 years training after a M.D. degree and denotes a non-surgical specialist.

FRCS[C] abbreviated title for Fellow of the Royal College of Surgeons. [C] represents Canadian College. Requires a further 4 years training after a M.D. degree.

Gastroenterologist Physician specializing in the digestive system: esophagus, stomach, and bowels.

Geneticist Specialist in genetic diseases – hereditary disorders and abnormalities.

Geriatrician Specialist in the diagnoses and treatment of illnesses in older people.

GI (Gastrointestinal) Series An x-ray examination of the esophagus, stomach, colon and rectum.

gm. abbrev. = grams.

gr. abbrev. = grains.

gtt. abbrev. = drops.

h abbrev. = hour.

Hematologist Physician specializing in conditions of the blood.

Hematoma Swelling caused by bleeding into tissues as in a bruise.

Hemiplegia One-sided paralysis of the body, usually from a stroke. A right-sided paralysis indicates left-sided brain damage.

Hemoglobin The protein in red blood cells that carry oxygen to the body tissues.

Hemorrhage Extensive abnormal bleeding.

Hereditary Something inherited from parents.

High Blood Pressure See Hypertension.

Hodgkin's Disease A form of lymphoid cancer that has high fever, enlarged lymph nodes and spleen, liver and kidneys and a dangerously lowered resistance to infection.

Hormone A glandular excretion into the blood that stimulates another organ.

Hospice Institution where palliative care is given to people with a terminal illness. Programs often have major homecare component and may also be part of an established institution such as a hospital.

h.s. abbrev. = at bedtime, before retiring. From the Latin hora somni.

Huntington's Chorea A hereditary condition with symptoms of uncontrolled movements and progressive mental disorder.

Hypertension High arterial blood pressure with no apparent symptoms; can lead to a stroke, heart failure or other serious condition if not treated. The pressure measures the force of the blood expelled from the heart against the walls of the blood vessels.

Hypnotic A drug used to induce sleep.

Hypnotism A diagnostic or pschotherapeutic treatment to put a patient into a sleeplike trance that enhances memory or makes the person susceptible to suggestion. Can be used in pain relief and to eliminate some negative habits.

Hypotension Low arterial blood pressure.

I&O abbrev. = intake and output refers to fluids into and out of body.

Iatrogenic Disease A condition caused by a physician.

ICU Intensive Care Unit within a hospital where seriously ill or post-operative patients receive intensified care.

Incontinence Lack of bladder or rectal control.

in d abbrev. = daily. From the Latin in dies.

Infarction Blockage of a blood vessel especially the artery leading to the heart.

Infection Inflammation or disease caused when bacteria, viruses and other micro-organisims invade the body.

Inflammation Swelling or irritation of tissue.

Insomnia An inability to sleep.

Intern An advanced student or recent medical school graduate undergoing supervised practical training.

Internist Physician who specializes in the nonsurgical treatment of the internal organs of the body.

IV abbrev. = intravenous in which a needle is kept within a vein for the injection of medication.

Laxative A drug to induce bowel movements.

Leukemia Cancer of white blood cells in which these cells reproduce abnormally and inhibit red cell formation.

Liabilities Debts owed to others such as a loan, mortgage, utility bills, credit card payments etc.

Lumbar Puncture A diagnostic procedure in which a hollow needle is inserted between two lumbar vertebrae in the spinal cord to remove some spinal fluid.

Lymph Glands Nodes of tissue that provide a system of protection against bacteria and other attacks against the body's immune system.

m et n abbrev. = morning and night.

Malignant Progressive or terminal condition.

Malnutrition Insufficient consumption of essential food elements whether by improper diet or illness.

Mammography An x-ray of the breasts to detect presence of tumors and whether tumor is malignant or benign.

Meningitis Inflammation of the membranes covering and protecting the brain and spinal cord.

Metastasis The spreading of an infection or cancer from it's original area to others throughout the body.

mg. abbrev. = milligrams.

mor dict abbrev. = in the manner directed.

Multiple Sclerosis A degenerative disease of the central nervous system in which the tissues harden.

Muscular Dystrophy A degenerative muscular disease in which muscles waste away.

Neoplasm A tumor or a new growth of abnormal tissue that has uncontrolled cell multiplication. See Cancer.

Nephrologist Physician specializing in kidney conditions.

Neurologist Physician specializing in the nervous system.

Neurosurgeon Physician specializing in surgery of the nervous system.

non rep abbrev. = do not repeat.

notarize A notary public authenticates or attests to the truth of a document (i.e. attests that a document was signed by a particular person).

notary public A public officer (can be a lawyer) who certifies documents, takes affidavits and administers oaths.

Nurse Practitioner Registered Nurse who has received additional training in order to perform more specialized medical care than other nurses.

o abbrev. = none.

Obstetrician/Gynecologist Physician specializing in conditions of the female reproductive system. Obstetrician specializes in pregnancies and births.

Oncologist Physician specializing in tumors and cancer.

Ophthalmologist Physician who specializes in diseases of the eye.

Optician Non-physician trained in filling prescriptions for eyeglasses and contact lens.

Optometrist Non-physician trained to measure vision and make eyeglasses and contact lens.

Orthopedist Physician specializing in bones.

Osteopathy The diagnoses and treatment of disorders by manipulative therapy, drugs, surgery, proper diet and psychothereapy to prevent disease and restore health. Not approved in all jurisdictions but where permitted, must be licensed.

Osteoporosis A weakening of the bones through a loss of calcium and occurs most often in old age.

Otolaryngologist A specialist in conditions of the ear, throat and nose.

Palliative Care Treatment to relieve symptoms, rather than cure, a disease or condition. In modern sense includes the physical, emotional and spiritual care of patients. Also called hospice care.

Paracentesis Fluid drainage by insertion of a tube into the body.

Parkinson's Disease A progressive nervous disease of the latter years. Symptoms are muscular tremor, slowing of movement, partial facial paralysis and impaired motor control.

Pathologist Physician who examines tissue and bone to diagnose if malignancy exists. They also perform autopsies.

Pathology The scientific study of disease.

pc abbrev. = after meals.

Pediatrician Physician specializing in the care of children.

pH Test Determines the degree of acidity or alkalinity in urine.

Physiatrist Physician specializing in rehabilitive therapy after illness or injury. Uses exercise, massage, water and heat to restoring useful activities to a person.

Physician A medical doctor as opposed to doctors with a Ph.D.

Placebo A substance containing no medication. It can help a patient who believes that it will work. A practical and effective treatment for some people.

Plasma The liquid part of blood (55% of total volume).

Plastic Surgeon Physician specializing in reconstructive surgery such as victims of major accidents.

Pneumonia An acute or chronic disease which inflames the lungs with associated fluid collection.

p.o. abbrev. = by mouth. From the Latin per os.

Podiatrist Non-physician who specializes in the care, treatment and surgery of feet.

prn abbrev. = as needed, as often as necessary.

Proctologist Physician specializing in diagnoses and treatment of disorders and diseases of anus, colon and rectum.

Prognosis (Prog.) A prediction of the future course of a condition or illness based upon scientific study. It is only a prediction and should not be accepted as fact.

Prosthesis An artificial substitute for a part of our body such as an arm or leg.

Psychiatrist Physician who specializes in the diagnosis and treatment of emotional and medical disorders; may prescribe medication.

Psychologist A professional with a Ph.D. in psychology who diagnoses and treats pyschological disorders. They may not prescribe medication.

pt abbrev. = patient.

Px abbrev. = prognosis.

q abbrev. = every.

q.h. abbrev. = every hour. From the Latin quaque hora.

q.i.d. abbrev. = four times a day. From the Latin quater in die.

qn abbrev. = every night. From the Latin quaque nox.

qod abbrev. = every other day.

qs abbrev. = proper amount, quantity sufficient.

Quack Opportunist who uses highly questionable or worthless methods or devices in diagnosing and treating various diseases.

ql abbrev. = as much as desired. From the Latin quantum libet.

Radiologist Physician who interprets X-rays. Sub-specialties include nuclear medicine and angiography.

Radiology A branch of science using radiant energy, as in x-rays, especially in the diagnosis and treatment of disease.

Regimen A program or set of rules to follow for treatment of a condition.

rep abbrev. = repeat.

Resident Physician receiving specialized clinical training.

Respirologist Specialist who diagnoses and treats diseases of lungs and respiratory (breathing) system.

Rheumatologist Specialist who diagnoses and treats rheumatic diseases characterized by inflammation or pain in the joints and muscles.

Rx abbrev. = prescription or therapy.

Senility Loss of mental ability and memory (especially of recent events). Age related deterioration of brain cells.

Shiatsu See Acupressure.

Shock Sudden, acute failure of body's circulatory function.

sig abbrev. = write, let it be imprinted.

Spinal Tap See Lumbar Puncture.

stat abbrev. = right away, immediately. From the Latin statim.

Stroke (Apoplexy) Sudden loss of muscular control, sensation and consciousness resulting from rupture or blocking of a blood vessel in the brain.

Suppository A medication given in solid form and inserted into the rectum or vagina. Disolves into a liquid by body heat.

Surgeon Physician who treats a disease by surgical operations. Surgeons generally specialize in one or more types of surgery.

Symptom An indication of a certain condition or disease.

Syndrome A group of symptoms that indicate a specific disease or condition.

Temperature Normal oral temperature is 97-99 degrees Fahrenheit or 36-37.2 degrees Celsius. Changes +/- one degree during day.

Thoracic Surgeon Physician who specializes in chest surgery.

t.i.d. abbrev. = three times a day. From the Latin tres in die.

Syndrome A group of symptoms that indicate a specific disease or condition.

Temperature Normal oral temperature is 97-99 degrees Fahrenheit or 36-37.2 degrees Celsius. Changes +/- one degree during day.

Thoracic Surgeon Physician who specializes in chest surgery.

t.i.d. abbrev. = three times a day. From the Latin tres in die.

Toxin A poison or harmful agent.

Tumor See Neoplasm.

Tx abbrev. = treatment.

Ultrasound Scan A picture of internal organs by using high frequency sound waves.

Urologist Physicians specializing in urinary tract and male prostrate gland diseases plus male sexual dysfunction. Although they treat non-surgical patients they also operate on kidneys and do prostate resectioning/removal.

ut dict abbrev. = as directed.

Vascular Surgeon Physician specializing in blood vessel surgery.

Vital Signs Measurement of temperature, pulse and respiration rate.

Vomiting A reflex action that contracts the stomach and ejects contents through the mouth.

X-ray Electromagnetic radiation used to create photographic pictures of the body's internal structures.

X-ray Dye A substance injected into a vein prior to an X-ray to highlight an area for examination. May cause an allergic reaction.

INDEX